The Adventures of a Conscript

The Adventures of a Conscript

of a Conscript

Annotated Second Edition

BY

W. H. Younce

Late 58th N.C.

With Notes and Annotations By
Matthew W. Younce

FIRST EDITION
THE EDITOR PUBLISHING COMPANY
CINCINNATI, OHIO
1901

ANNOTATED SECOND EDITION
YOUNCE BOOKS
FREDERICKSBURG, VIRGINIA
2022

Younce Books
Fredericksburg, Virginia

Softcover ISBN: 979-8-3683-1730-4
Hardcover ISBN: 979-8-3715-0110-3

14   13   12   11   10   9   8   7   6   5   4

ACKNOWLEDGEMENTS

Of course, thanks to W. H. for writing this book, and more importantly, for following his conscience.

Additionally, I am grateful to the following people for their assistance in my research:

Linda Talley, the Genealogy Librarian at the *Johnson County Museum of History, Franklin, Indiana,* went above and beyond in sending me photos, maps, articles, and information about W. H.'s life after he settled in Franklin, Indiana.

Anne Mason, the Executive Director of the *Jonesborough/ Washington County History Museum and Archives, operated by the Heritage Alliance, Jonesborough, Tennessee,* graciously provided a photo of the courthouse and additional information about it for inclusion in this book.

Bev Repass Hoch, the Director of the *Wythe County Genealogical and Historical Association,* was very helpful in providing information on the site of Toland's Raid in Wytheville, as well as generously locating photographs of Wytheville from the time of the battle.

FOREWORD

I first discovered the existence of this book in the 1990s. I typed my last name into the newly available World Wide Web and found that almost a century before, someone named William Younce had written a book about his experiences in the Civil War. I thought it was interesting, and I was sure he was somehow related to me.

Fast forward to 2020, when the pandemic sent many of us home. I began working on my family tree to pass the time and learned a lot about my family's history.

The first recorded reference to a member of my family in America was an immigrant on a ship that arrived from Germany in 1738. Wilhelm Janß[1] arrived in Philadelphia on the ship Winter Galley.

The next reference in the records is to Johannes Jans, who was likely Wilhelm's son. Johannes was born in 1760 and baptized in 1786, along with his wife Margaretha, at the Moravian Church in Friedberg, North Carolina. In 1799, property records show that Johannes purchased land along the New River in Ashe County.

He is mentioned several times in the *Records of the Moravians in North Carolina*, including this passage from 1802:

> "I wanted to go to the home of a *John Jans*, who formerly belonged to the congregation of Friedberg, but the New River must be crossed four times to reach his house, and because of the continuous rain the water was so high that I had to give it up. I heard that he had gone over to the Baptists and had been re-baptized."[2]

_____

[1] The eszett (ß) in German represents an 'ss' sound. In English, especially typewritten, it may be written with an s, ss, or sz.

[2] Source: https://archive.org/details/recordsofthemora06frie/page/2966/mode/2up

Johannes and Margaretha had several children, and by the early 1800s, the family began spelling the name Younce, while retaining the original pronunciation, which rhymes with "sconce" and not "bounce."[3]

One of Johannes and Margaretha's children, Johannes Jr., married a woman named Sarah. They had several children, including a son named David. David married Lois Perkins, and they had several children, one of whom was William Henry, the author of this book, born in 1842.

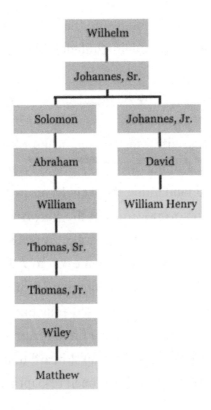

FAMILY TREE FROM WILHELM JANß TO THE AUTHORS

---

[3] The IPA pronunciation is /jɑːns/, not /jaʊns/.

I am also a direct descendant of Johannes and Margaretha, through another one of their sons, Solomon Younce. Johannes and Margaretha are my 5th-great-grandparents, making William my second cousin, four times removed. Admittedly, this is a rather distant relationship. However, knowing that I could officially see I was related to the author made me more interested in what he wrote in his book.

Continuing my research, I learned that William went by W. H. and was occasionally nicknamed "Buck." I then found a scanned copy of the book. Although it was faded and hard to read in some parts, I could make out the text.

As I began reading, I found myself captivated by the story, regardless of the fact that he was my cousin. I was deeply interested in his account and gained new insights into the mindset of some Southerners during the Civil War.

Decades after the war ended, around the turn of the last century, Confederate "heritage" groups began erecting statues and memorials to Confederate soldiers across the South. Roads, buildings, schools, and even entire towns and counties, were named after Confederates. These statues and names aimed to rewrite history and portray the Confederates in a positive light. However, the "Lost Cause" myth of the Confederacy's supposedly noble reasons for existence is exactly that—a myth.

I wonder if W. H.'s decision to write his memoir was in response to this rewriting of history. Or perhaps he was just someone who wanted to tell a good story? Whatever his motivation, I am grateful that he put pen to paper.

In recent years, our country has undergone changes. Confederate monuments and street signs have been removed, and with them, some of my previous understanding of the War Between the States has also come down.

Growing up, I frequently heard the term "States' Rights." It was said that states had the right to determine their own destiny, laws, and culture. The argument was made that before the war, the phrase was "The United States are..." while after, it became "The United States is..." due to the loss of individuality among the states. I heard repeatedly how Robert E. Lee could have led the Union Army, but he remained loyal to his state, Virginia, and thus fought for it.

While reading this book, I encountered my cousin's own words that challenged my previous understanding of the war. I read with pride as my cousin proclaimed himself an American. It didn't matter that he was from North Carolina. He clearly stated that his allegiance to the Stars and Stripes was far greater than any allegiance to his state. Importantly, he directly attributed slavery as the reason for the war, debunking the nebulous "States' Rights" philosophy.

I continued my research on the book and W. H.'s life, with the intention of reprinting this book for others to read, I hope you enjoy it.

Now, I present the text of W. H. Younce's "The Adventures of a Conscript" exactly as it was originally written over 120 years ago, with only a few additions:

- Contextual Footnotes: I added notes to provide context or additional information about the story. For example, for any soldier W. H. mentioned, I tried to determine his identity, usually based on information from the National Park Service's Soldiers and Sailors Database.[4]

- Images: Before this book was printed in one volume, W. H. published it as a series of eight installments in The National Tribune, a veterans' newspaper. Each article was accompanied by a sketch of a scene. I have included these sketches in their respective places in the story. I have also included some historical photos of the sites he describes.

- Appendix: Additional information about W. H. and his family that I discovered during my research for this book is included here, in the hope that it will be of interest to the reader.

- Map: A map showing the locations mentioned in the book is included to allow the reader to follow W. H.'s adventures.here. I hope this will be of interest to the reader.

Matthew W. Younce
Fredericksburg, Virginia

---

[4] Source: https://www.nps.gov/civilwar/search-soldiers.htm

THE ADVENTURES OF A CONSCRIPT

In the northwestern county[5] of North Carolina between the Allegheny Mountains[6] on the west and the Blue Ridge on the east, nestled among the hills is the home of the writer previous to the outbreak of the Civil War.

There I first saw the light of day in a country as beautiful as any in Italy or Switzerland. Often in my childhood I have watched on the summit of the grand old mountains, and have seen the spirit of the storm take his evening naps in his pavilion of darkness and again I have listened to the songs of the birds as they mingled their tunes with the low hum of the mountain brooks. There amidst these conditions and surroundings I grew to young manhood and many lessons were derived from nature that proved of much value in later years.

Although with limited opportunities for obtaining an education on account of the primitive schools that existed in that country, I had been more fortunate than many other young men who had grown up with me. From early childhood I had been a close student and an earnest seeker after knowledge. I believed it was

---

[5] Ashe County, North Carolina, situated on the North Carolina-Tennessee and North Carolina-Virginia borders, had been the home of four generations of the Younce family, beginning with Johannes and Margaretha Jans who moved there in 1799.

[6] This is referring to the entire mountain range we now call the Appalachians. "Allegheny" and "Appalachian" were used interchangeably as the name of the mountain chain until 1907, when the U. S. Board on Geographic Names officially approved Appalachian for the mountain range's name..

possible in this great country of ours for a man of ambition to reach a higher and nobler life than those who were content to grow up and fall like the leaves.

I had completed the common grades and was ready to enter upon higher branches when the call to arms came. In politics I had been trained in the old Whig[7] school, and although, on account of my youth, I had taken but little interest in affairs of Government, living in the midst of slavery, and daily observing the evils of the whole system, I had become thoroughly imbued with the anti-slavery doctrine, and every day was more and more convinced in my own mind that it was wrong.

When, in 1860, Mr. Lincoln was elected President, I then heard the mutterings of secession and the boast that one Southern man was equal to ten "Yankees." In a short time one State after another followed in rapid succession, severing the ties that held them together.[8]

---

[7] The Whigs were an American political party from the 1830s - 1850s. The party favored limiting Presidential power, and opposed the Democratic Party. While the party did not take a position on slavery, it was generally anti-slavery, especially in the North.

[8] After Abraham Lincoln was elected president on November 6, 1860, eleven states seceded from the Union, between December 1860 and June 1861. In order, they are: South Carolina, Mississippi, Florida, Alabama, Georgia, Louisiana, Texas, Virginia, Arkansas, North Carolina, and Tennessee.

EARLIER DAYS OF THE WAR

Throughout the whole South we heard martial music, the fervent appeals of the orator, the tramp of the young soldier, the plaudits of the multitude as they marched away to the struggle under the new flag. To see so many of my associates proudly marching to the war in a blaze of glory was a great temptation to me, and often I implored Divine Providence that, if I was wrong in my political conviction, to give me understanding, and place me right. I was ready and willing to fight for my country under the old flag, but could never consent that my weapon should be drawn in what I believed to be an unworthy cause.

The summer of 1861 dragged slowly on. I had become intensely interested, and was watching every movement of the two armies. My faith was unshaken in the superiority and strategy of Northern arms, when suddenly, on the 21st of July, the news flashed throughout the country of the defeat of the Union army at Bull Run.[9] The whole South was electrified, and we heard nothing but the triumphant shout of the victors and the boast of Southern chivalry.

By this time, beardless boy though I was, I had been marked and spotted as a "Lincolnite," "a Yankee sympathizer," and a "traitor." The Fall and Winter of '61 to '62 passed slowly on, and I began to realize that I must suppress my convictions on the issues of the war, though my faith grew stronger on the side of the North.

---

[9] First Battle of Bull Run, in Manassas, Virginia, July of 1861.

With the opening of Spring renewed energy was put forth to strengthen the cause and increase the army, and by June about all the available volunteers had been mustered into service, and as I looked at the situation at this time, in my soul there was rejoicing. Fort Donelson had fallen, and the Union army had more than held its own at Shiloh.[10] New hopes shone blazing before my vision. General McClellan was marching on to Richmond with that grand army of 100,000 men. I fully believed that Richmond would fall; that no power there could impede the progress of that great army. Again the friends of the Union were doomed to disappointment, for McClellan was defeated, and forced to retire.[11]

The climax was now reached. Those in sympathy with the Southern cause grew still more arrogant, and no one's life and property were safe if it was known he was in sympathy with the Union.

---

[10] Fort Donelson and Shiloh were Union victories in western Tennessee in early 1862.

[11] Confederate victories in the Seven Days Battles of Virginia in June-July 1862 led to McClellan being replaced by U. S. Grant as the head of the Union Army.

CONFEDERATE CONSCRIPT LAW

About this time the Confederate Congress passed the wholesale conscript law,[12] including every one between the ages of eighteen and forty-five, and as I had just reached my twentieth year, it was then my real trouble began. It was then I began casting about to find some way of escape. About the 1st of August myself and three other companions, under the leadership of a good old Baptist preacher, started on horseback through East Tennessee with the purpose of reaching Kentucky and the Union army. After several weeks' scouting and maneuvering we found we could not make our escape by that mode of travel, and in September returned to our home. The Governor of my State[13] had issued a proclamation ordering all conscripted men to report on a certain day at their respective Countyseats for duty, and failing to do so they were to be arrested as deserters. The militia between the ages of thirty-five and forty-five were ordered into camp in their respective Counties to enforce the conscript law. On the 5th day of October they were in camp about a mile from my father's home.

The scenes of which I am now about to describe will never be forgotten while life lasts. The militia was regularly organized, and under the command of Colonel Gentry.[14] My father's family

---

[12] The Confederate States' Second Conscription Act was enacted September 27, 1862.

[13] Zebulon B. Vance, who was personally against conscription, but was compelled to follow North Carolina state law.

[14] Colonel Allen Gentry was the leader of the Ashe County Militia.

consisted of father and mother and myself and one brother three years my senior.[15] On that day he and I and two other companions mounted our horses and started for Tennessee, the State line being but six miles west. The people of that part of Tennessee being extremely loyal to the Union, and there being no soldiers in that country, we felt comparatively safe among our friends there. We crossed the State line late in the evening just as the shadows of the tall peaks around us were climbing the sides of the mountains over in the east. A short distance beyond the State line, in the edge of Tennessee, lived a family whom I will call Carroll, consisting of father, mother, and three daughters. They were the only family for miles around, save one or two, whose sympathies were with the Southern cause. I will not attempt to describe the personnel of the Carroll girls, but will only say they were noted for their beauty for miles around.

I had been a frequent visitor at their home for some months previous to this, paying my attentions to Miss Edith, the youngest of the three sisters. She and I had often talked of the issues of the war. She was extremely loyal to the South, and believed, as did thousands of other Southern people, the Yankees would not fight; that they were an inferior and cowardly race, and that one Southern man was more than equal to five of them. She used all the persuasive powers at her command to influence me to volunteer in

---

[15] Father: David, Mother: Lois (née Perkins), Brother: Calvin.
Although unmentioned, W. H. also has sisters Minerva, Sarah, Nancy, and Susan. See the appendix for more details.

the Confederate army, but I always met her arguments with my side of the question, and her influence proved of no avail.

THE ADVENTURES OF A CONSCRIPT

AN UNFORTUNATE DECISION

On the evening above referred to, as the road passed near the door of her home, it occurred to me to stop and remain over night. I so stated my intentions to my companions. Each of them vigorously entered his protest against it, and used all the arguments he could command to have me go on with them about four miles farther down the country, among friends, where we would be safe. It was of no use, however. I designated the place I would meet them next morning at eight o'clock. I dismounted, entered the house, and my companions went on. My horse, as usual, was taken to the barn.

Miss Edith expressed some surprise at my visit just at that time, but I carelessly turned it off, saying I was going down in the country to be gone a few days, and it was quite convenient for me to come this far on my journey this evening. She knew nothing of the real cause of my unexpected appearance, and it was a question in my mind as to whether I ought to tell her or not. After supper she invited me to the parlor, and she at once began to talk of the war, saying she had understood that over in my State, all conscripted men were being arrested as deserters; that the militia was in camp and scouring the country for conscripts.

"Your information is correct," said I.

"Then, sir, perhaps I can surmise the cause of your unexpected visit this evening," she retorted. "But, oh, no; it can't be possible that you are fleeing for refuge! You can not only be turning your back upon your own country in the darkest hour of its peril, but by

8

this act blasting every hope for an honorable and useful life in the future, to which you have always aspired! O, if I were only a man, how I would teach you a lesson in patriotism by shouldering my musket and marching to the front!"

"Miss Edith," said I, "you talk very prettily, and grow quite eloquent, but you represent a wicked and unjust cause. Your surmise is correct. I am fleeing for refuge, and know not where I will find safety. The Government to which you refer so eloquently is not my country. I owe my allegiance to that country only that is represented by that beautiful emblem of the free, the Stars and Stripes. It is true this is my native land, and I love its mountains, but I cannot and will not fight for a Government that seeks to enslave me, and whose cornerstone is slavery."

"Yes," said she; "but what will you do? You cannot escape. Besides, you are risking your life in the attempt."

"I know," said I, "the last statement is true. There are men in my country who would be cowardly and mean enough to take my life; but my purpose is to try to escape, and get to the Union army, and I have faith that, if the God in whom I trust notices even the fall of a sparrow, He will deliver me from the hands of my enemies. And, now, Miss Edith, I have made a clean breast of it to you as to my purpose for the future. In the morning I will bid you good-by having perfect confidence that you will not betray me until I am beyond the reach of all those who would do me harm."

"It grieves me," said she, "that you have determined on this course, but I assure you that, come what may, no word or deed of mine shall ever do you harm. I will shield and protect you so far as it is in my power to do," and laying her hand on my arm, and the tears welling up in her eyes, she said: "As you are determined on this course, I pray that God will guide you, and that you may safely reach your destination beyond the reach of your enemies."

A NIGHT SURPRISE

It was now between nine and ten o'clock, and time to retire for the night. I went to my room, and had just got comfortably settled in bed and began to wonder what another day would bring, when suddenly I heard the rattling of horses' hoofs on the stony highway. My heart leaped to my throat. My first impulse was to spring from my bed and try to make my escape from the house, and then, not knowing whether or not there was real danger, I thought that would be cowardly. Nearer and nearer they approached, when suddenly they halted in front of the house. I knew then that it was too late, and I at once began to try to nerve myself for whatever might happen. In less time than it takes to tell it they had surrounded the house and were making an alarm at the front door.

They were admitted by Mr. Carroll. I heard the question asked if I was there, which was answered in the affirmative. I then arose and began to dress myself, and when I was dressed walked into the room.

Major Long[16] (for that was his name) laid his hand on my shoulder and said :

"Sir, you are my prisoner."

"I acknowledge your authority, Major, and realize that I am," I replied.

At this moment Miss Edith came dashing down the stairway, her long, dark hair hanging loosely over her shoulders, and in a fit

---

[16] George Washington Long, leader of the Home Guard of Ashe County.

of excitement began to plead with Major Long to tell her what he was going to do with me.

"Young lady, you seem to be very much interested in this young man," he replied, "and I say to you that he is unworthy of your recognition, much less of your confidence and friendship. He is a traitor to his country, and deserves no mercy at our hands."

At this remark the hot blood mounted to my forehead, and straightening myself to my full height I said:

"Sir, that is an insult. I stand here helpless, your prisoner, and no one but a coward would insult a prisoner. ""

At this he seized me roughly by the shoulder.

"Sir," said he, "I would advise you to be careful how you talk. You are insane, or perhaps worse, in love" (pointing his finger at Miss Edith), "I know not which: but I do know you are not in love with your country. We will now change your occupation, and put you at something else besides riding over the country and shouting for Lincoln."

"Yes, sir," said I. "I am in love with — Liberty."

By this time my horse was ready. I bade Miss Edith good-by, and we hurried from the house. Mounting our horses we started back toward North Carolina. After going perhaps a mile we came to where the road passed through a long gap in the mountain, and Major Long ordered the men to stop, saying they would remain there and guard the road through the night, and capture any others who might try to escape by this route. We dismounted, and I was carefully guarded till daylight. Major Long had seven men with

"Yes, sir," said I. "I am in love with — liberty."

FROM THE NATIONAL TRIBUNE, NOV. 23, 1899

him. Some one, though I never knew who it was, had passed the Carroll home and seen me stop there, and going over into North Carolina had met Major Long and his men, and reported me, and they at once started for their game.

With the dawn of the morning we started for camp, six or seven miles to the east. We passed near my home, but the Major refused to allow me to stop. When we arrived at camp a guard was detailed to take charge of me. A brother of Colonel Gentry, whom I have before mentioned, was Captain of Company L in the 58th North Carolina.[17] He was at home on recruiting service, and was with the militia. They had proposed to all conscripts who would voluntarily surrender themselves the privilege of volunteering in Captain Gentry's[18] company. About fifty, through intimidation and fear, had reported and volunteered. I sent word to my father that I had been

---

[17] "The 58th Infantry Regiment was organized in July of 1862 in Mitchell County, North Carolina, and made up of members from Mitchell, Yancey, Watauga, Caldwell, McDowell, and Ashe counties. In September it moved to Cumberland Gap and spent the winter of 1862-1863 at Big Creek Gap, near Jacksboro, Tennessee. During the war it was assigned to Kelly's, Reynolds', Brown's and Reynolds' Consolidated, and Palmer's Brigade. The 58th participated in the campaigns of the Army of Tennessee from Chickamauga to Atlanta, guarded prisoners at Columbia, Tennessee, during Hood's operations, then moved to South Carolina and skirmished along the Edisto River. Later it returned to North Carolina and saw action at Bentonville. It lost 46 killed and 114 wounded at Chickamauga, totaled 327 men and 186 arms in December, 1863, and took about 300 to Bentonville. The unit was included in the surrender April 26, 1865."

Source: https://www.nps.gov/civilwar/search-battle-units-detail.htm?battleUnitCode=CNC0058RI

[18] Captain William H. Gentry appears on the Company L roster.

captured, and to come for my horse. I fully expected to go to our county seat and be incarcerated in jail until they were ready to send me to the front at Richmond.

The time passed slowly on. It was a sad day for me. Many of my rebel friends came and took me by the hand, and expressed great sympathy for me, saying they were very sorry I had taken such an unwise step. They said I had missed the opportunity of my life; that my aspirations ought to have led me to have entered the army; that I could have had a commission.

These were the stories that were poured into my ears by those who pretended to be my friends. During the day father and mother had come and had been permitted to see me and say good-by, and then returned to their home heartbroken with grief. Late in the afternoon, Colonel Gentry, Captain Gentry, and another friend of mine came to me and proposed that if I would take the oath of allegiance to the Southern cause, volunteer in Captain Gentry's company, take charge of fifty recruits, and conduct them to the regiment, they would allow me to do so, and would not send me away as a conscript or deserter.

After talking the matter over for some time, I agreed to do so, thinking as they already had me, that was the best thing I could do. The oath was administered by Colonel Gentry, and my name was enrolled on the company's books.[19] All this occurred while I was a

---

[19] William H. Younce enlisted in Company L of the 58th North Carolina Infantry on July 20, 1862. Source: North Carolina. Division of Archives and History. North Carolina Troops 1861-1865 A Roster. 14 vols., Raleigh: University Graphics, 1993.

prisoner, but immediately afterward I was released, with permission to go to my home to remain over night, and with orders to report next morning at eight o'clock for duty, to start to the regiment.

There was surprise at my home that evening when I arrived. I told them the turn things had taken, and we discussed the question as to whether or not the oath I had taken under the circumstances was binding. I was of the opinion that it was not, but I finally decided there was nothing left for me to do at that time but to go, and wait my opportunity to make my escape at some future time. It was a night of agony for me, and I slept but little, and next morning I again said good-by, and reported for duty.

There were just fifty recruits, including myself, and all were ready to start. The people from the country around were there to say good-by to the boys. I was the hero of the occasion, and the crowd became so enthusiastic that I was carried on the shoulders of some of the younger men to a platform and forced to make a short talk. The people thought that I had repented, and, "there was more rejoicing over one sinner that repented than over ninety and nine that went not astray."[20] They could not read my thoughts. My purposes were the same, and I believed that I would find refuge under the flag of my country some day.

It was now time to start, and after the good-byes had all been said to the weeping mothers, wives, sisters and children, I lined the

---

[20] Paraphrased from Luke 15:7.

men up in double file and gave the order to march. It was forty miles to the railroad, but nothing unusual happened during our journey, and in one week from the day we started we joined the regiment, then at Tazewell, Tenn. We were immediately mustered into the service. Then, as we settled down to the ordinary camp life, after the exciting scenes of the last ten days, I had plenty of time for reflection.

At times I grew melancholy and despondent. There was a great burden on my soul. I had registered an oath in Heaven that I would never fight for the Southern cause, and bear arms against my country, and in the bitterness of my remorse I cried out: "Why did not my tongue cleave to the roof of my mouth before taking the oath of allegiance to the Jeff Davis Government? Why did I not let them take my life?"

I talked to three of my companions whom I could trust, and began to devise some means by which we might yet make our escape, and after several days' planning and consulting, we decided to desert, go back to the mountains at our home, and wait for the nearer approach of the Union army, and then make a last desperate attempt to get inside the Union lines.

THE ADVENTURES OF A CONSCRIPT

DESERTING FROM THE ARMY

So, after having been in camp about two weeks, about the first of November, on Thursday afternoon, we flanked the guards and soon found ourselves in the country among the hills, The names of the three men with me were Robinson,[21] Roark,[22] and Reedy,[23] all several years my senior. That evening when night came, we left the woods and took the road. We traveled all night, and when morning came went into the woods.

We continued our journey during the day, but made slow progress through the rough mountains, and when night came we were so worn out for want of rest and sleep that we lay down on the cold ground on the mountainside among the pines, with no covering save the canopy of Heaven, and slept soundly until morning. Before leaving camp we had taken the precaution to prepare food to last us a day or two, which we smuggled out when we left, and on the morning referred to we had enough for a scanty breakfast.

This was on Saturday, and we started on our journey feeling much refreshed. We made good progress that day, traveling along the mountain paths and by-roads, and felt reasonably secure, but as night began to come on we grew tired and hungry, having had nothing to eat since morning, and but little then. Still, we traveled

---

[21] Benjamin F. Robinson appears on the Company L roster.

[22] Joshua, Solomon, and William Roark appear on the Company L roster.

[23] George W. Reedy appears on the Company L roster.

on until darkness had settled down upon us. We then left the woods, and sought the road.

We were dragging our weary limbs along, wondering how much further we could go that night, when we saw a light in a farm house some distance from the road. We were so tired and hungry we thought there could be no harm in going to the house, asking for supper, and remaining over night. Besides, we knew there were many Union people through this part of the country, and we would simply take our chances It was a desperate chance, as will be seen further on.

Leaving the main road we walked over to the house. It was a large frame residence with porch running the entire length of the front, having the appearance of a place whose owner might be in good circumstances. We were cordially received, and told that supper would be prepared for us, and that we were welcome to remain over night. After a short time supper was announced. We were conducted to the dining-room, and as we were all unusually hungry we enjoyed the meal very much. The gentleman told us his name was Wood, and that he never turned any one from his home hungry, He asked us to what command we belonged. We told him the 58th N.C. and that we were going home on a thirty days' leave of absence. He, observing that we were tired and sleepy, suggested that we had better retire, to which we readily agreed. We were conducted to a large bed-room adjoining the sitting-room, containing two beds, and when left alone were soon in bed and asleep. We were so tired and exhausted we slept soundly till morning, when we were aroused by an alarm at our room door, saying it was time to get up for breakfast.

ARRESTED AS DESERTERS

We arose, dressed ourselves, and when we were all ready to go out found the door locked. When we were heard, it was immediately opened, however, and to our horror we looked into the muzzles of half a dozen muskets in the hands of as many Confederate soldiers. Our genial host stepped toward us and said: "Gentlemen, you are my prisoners."

My heart almost stood still. It seemed that my very breath was gone. I stood for some time speechless, and my muscles refused to move. Mr. Wood broke the silence.

"I am the Enrolling Officer," said he, "of this district. I believe you have deserted from the army, and whether you have or not, that makes no difference. You are either deserters or conscripts, and as such it becomes my duty, as a patriot and one who is loyal to his country, to arrest you and turn you over to the proper authorities. You told me last night you had a leave of absence; if so, produce it."

"Mr. Wood," said I, "we have nothing to produce. You have simply taken advantage of fatigue and hunger and we have fallen into your trap."

"When you came to my house last night," he said, "I felt sure that you were deserters. You were securely locked in, but you did not know it. Then I immediately dispatched messengers for these brave boys," pointing to the soldiers, "whom I knew would get here in time to capture you, and now, gentlemen, what have you to say?"

"Sir," said I, "we have nothing to say."

"Come, then," said he, "out on the porch, wash, and prepare for breakfast, I have ordered a good breakfast prepared for you, for you will need it in view of the trip you have before you."

We followed as he directed, the soldiers holding their guns in readiness for any emergency that might happen. When we had reached the porch near the corner of the house Roark and Reedy made a dash for liberty.

Quick as thought they dashed around the corner of the house, leaped over a low fence, and started across an open field toward a wood about two hundred yards away. The guards were on the alert, and four of them dashed around the corner after them, getting in plain view of them just as they were leaping the fence. I stepped to the corner just in time to see each guard place his gun to his shoulder, take deliberate aim, and fire. For a moment I held my breath, for I fully expected to see both boys fall, as they were not more than twenty-five yards from them; but strange to say, neither one of them was touched, and had they continued it is possible that they might have reached the wood and escaped. While the guards were re-loading they might have gotten beyond their reach; but they both stopped, turned around and came back. We then went into breakfast, while the guards stood in the room and at the door. We ate but little; in fact, Roark and Reedy, after their excitement, ate nothing, and when we were through, Wood had brought and prepared a lot of ropes with which to tie us. He said it was fifteen miles to Rogersville, and they would have to take us down there, and perhaps it would be best to tie us, and then we would be sure not to get away.

A guard was ready to tie each of the other three men, and Wood came to me and slipped a noose over one hand. I held my other hand from him, and said: "Sir, this is cruel. Why do you tie us? You are cowards, or you would not treat helpless prisoners in this way." Looking me in the eye, he hesitated, and said:

"If you will pledge your word of honor not to try to make your escape, we will not tie you."

"As for myself," said I, "I will make no pledge. You would not believe me if I did. Do as you please."

In the meantime he had slipped the rope from my hand, and after a private consultation with the officer of the Guard, they decided not to tie us.

By this time Wood's horse had been brought and saddled, and was standing with the horses of the soldiers, ready to start. We were ordered to go in front; they mounted the horses and rode close behind us, and our tramp of fifteen miles began.

We did fairly well for the first three or four miles, but our feet were sore and blistered, and they crowded us so closely that we soon began to fag. They would not allow us to go to the foot bridges that spanned the little streams, prepared for pedestrians, but forced us to wade all the streams in front of their horses, and we were soon wet to our bodies; and to add still further to our suffering, in the afternoon a wet, heavy snow begun to fall. We were almost given out, and, had I been permitted to have done so,

They forced us to wade the icy streams.

FROM THE NATIONAL TRIBUNE, NOV 30, 1899

would have lain down in the snow by the road side and remained there till death relieved me.

Slowly and painfully we dragged ourselves along, with the horses of the soldiers almost tramping us, till, just as darkness began to settle down upon us, we reached Rogersville.

THE ADVENTURES OF A CONSCRIPT

IN JAIL AT ROGERSVILLE

We went straight to the jail, and Wood instructed the jailer what disposition to make of us. He ordered him to put us in a cell and keep us there until the proper authorities from Knoxville should send for and take us down there for court-martial. He accompanied us upstairs, the jailer unlocked the cell door, and we walked in as directed, the door swung back in its place, and the great iron bolt clicked behind us. They then turned and left us in darkness, without a ray of light penetrating the dismal gloom. The cell, as I remember it, looking back through the intervening years, was about six by eight feet, and contained nothing save the cold bare floor. We had eaten nothing since morning, and were wet all over, having, as before stated, waded all the streams on our journey, and had been exposed all afternoon to the wet snow, which at this time was about four inches deep.

We lay down on the door or sat and leaned with our backs against the cold, iron grating to rest. There was no one of us who felt like talking. We were too tired and hungry; but after a while the jailer came up, bringing us some supper. It consisted of warm corn bread, fried bacon and water. We were so hungry we had no complaint to make at the bill of fare, and ate all he gave us.

After we had finished our meal, we passed back to him through the iron grating the tinware from which we had eaten our supper. He picked up his light and disappeared down the stairway leaving us again in total darkness.

O, the horrors and suffering of that night!

We were so cold it seemed that we would certainly freeze. We could not lie down, but kept moving around all night. One of the boys had grown melancholy. He said he would never get out of this trouble; they would court-martial us; we could make no defense; would be found guilty, and that meant death.

"That is true," said I, "but I tell you we will not be court-martialed. If the Confederate Government should court-martial and shoot all its deserters, it would decimate the army. It cannot afford to. They might possibly, for policy sake, make an example of some one, and we might be the ones, but I believe I will yet make my escape to the Union army. Just how I am to get out of this I don't know, but I believe there is some way out."

As the boys were feeling so despondent, I tried to cheer them up. I did not express to them my own feelings, for my mental anguish as well as my physical suffering was terrible. As I would stand and gaze into the black darkness that enveloped me it seemed that my very brain was whirling, and I would cling to the cold iron grating for support —

> "Deep into that darkness peering, long I stood there, wondering, fearing;
> Doubting, dreaming dreams no mortal ever dared to dream before."[24]

---

[24] From *The Raven,* by Edgar Allan Poe.

Finally, gathering all my strength, I shook off the despondency into which I had fallen, and thought:

"There was never a night without a day,
Or an evening without a morning."[25]

And there was another cheering thought that those on whose souls my misfortunes were the greatest burdens did not know where I was, and that I was suffering almost the agonies of death in that prison cell.

The long, dreary night dragged slowly on, and at last the gray streaks of the morning began to penetrate the iron-grated window. Our clothes had partly dried, and the cold was less severe.

About eight o'clock the jailer came up, bringing our breakfast, consisting of the same as our supper the night before. We enjoyed the meal, and, as before, ate all he brought.

While we were eating he sat down on a stool close to the cell door, and began talking about the war. After he had been talking a short time I gathered from his conversation that he was not in sympathy with the South. I then felt more free to talk to him. He said it was shameful and brutal to treat men as we were being treated. "But," said he, "Wood, who is known as one of the meanest rebels in all the country, had ordered you locked in this cell, and I have no alternative but to obey. But," said he, "I am

---

[25] From *The Golden Side*, by M.A. Kidder.

your friend, and you have my deepest sympathy, and if you will promise me that you will not try to escape, I will take you out of this cell, and let you go in another room across the hall, where there is a stove, and I will keep a fire for you, and make it as pleasant for you is I can; but, understand, I do this at my own risk, and if you should escape I would have to suffer for it."

"Kind friend," said I, "I thank you for the kind words you have spoken, and the sympathy you have expressed for us. You see our pitiable condition, and are familiar with the circumstances that have brought us here, and I assure you on our word of honor that if you will remove us from this cell that no act of ours shall ever bring trouble to you. Although we are here in a criminal's cell, we claim to be honorable gentlemen."

He turned and went down stairs, and in a few minutes returned with a bunch of keys in his hand. Thrusting one of them into the lock, the heavy bolt flew back, the great iron door swung open, and we walked out into the corridor of the jail.

We followed him as he directed, and found ourselves in a warm, comfortable room, even supplied with seats. This was on Monday morning, and this good man spent a portion of the day in the room with us, and when night came provided sufficient bed-clothes. He said: "You ought to have a good night's rest, for tomorrow they will be after you to take you to Knoxville, and I do not know how you will fare when you get there."

Night again settled down upon us, and as the last rays of the fading twilight shone feebly through the grated window, we

THE ADVENTURES OF A CONSCRIPT

prepared our bed on the floor, with the bed-clothing that had been furnished us by the jailor, and slept soundly through the night. Tuesday morning was clear and bright. When breakfast was brought, hot coffee had been added to our bill of fare instead of water. About ten o'clock a Lieutenant with four men made their appearance at the jail, saying he had come up from Knoxville with orders for four deserters that were confined here in jail. He was conducted to our room, and ordered us to be ready for the train in the afternoon. I said to him: "We are ready now; we have no preparations to make."

Just before train time, accompanied by the jailer and guard, he entered our room, and we at once started for the depot. Our good friend, the jailor, whose name I never knew, accompanied us to the station, and as we went aboard the train cordially bade each one of us good-by, and we were on our way to Knoxville, wondering what would be our doom.

TAKEN TO KNOXVILLE

The train was frequently delayed, and made slow time, and did not arrive at Knoxville till about eight o'clock at night.

We were immediately conducted to the Provost-Marshal's office. He was sitting at his desk when we walked in. The Lieutenant in charge saluted him, and reported four prisoners. The Captain (that was his rank, as I observed from the insignia he wore) arose from his seat and walked toward us.

"What is the charge, Lieutenant," he asked.

"Desertion," was the reply.

"That is a serious charge," said he. "Gentlemen, what have you to say?" he demanded with an oath, adding that it was strange that stout, able-bodied young men would desert to keep from fighting for their country, and he proceeded to deliver us a lecture as to our duty.

"Captain," said I, "when you are fully informed as to the facts in our case, you will perhaps feel differently. We are not deserters; we did not desert to keep from fighting for our country. We have been in the service more than a year, have seen perhaps more service than you have. We had never had nor asked for a leave of absence. We simply started to our homes, expecting to remain a few days, and then return to our regiment. We were not arrested by our own command, but by strangers who did not know us, and here we are under guard charged with desertion; and now, sir, we most humbly beg that you will allow us the privilege of returning to our regiment."

"What is your regiment?" He asked.

"The 58th N.C."

Said he: "You look like honest men, and I hope that your case is no worse than you have stated, but for to-night the only disposition I can make of you is to send you to jail," and turning to the Lieutenant, said: "You will see that these men are securely kept in jail till morning; when I will further investigate their case."

POLITICAL PRISONERS

That evening as we were coming down on the train, at a station up the road a fish vender boarded the train, and we bought from him a fish weighing over five or six pounds; and as we turned to leave the Marshal's office he asked us what we would take for that fish. I replied, "It is not for sale, but with the hope that you will think of us in the morning and take us out of jail, we will make you a present of it," and with that I handed it to him. He took it, but whether this had anything to do with his treatment of us afterward of course I never knew. We were then taken to the jail. It was more of a barracks than a prison, guarded on the outside by soldiers.

This jail has been more fully described than it is possible for me to do, by Parson Brownlow, in his book,[26] written after he had been incarcerated in it, and had been released and sent North. There were perhaps one hundred to one hundred and fifty prisoners confined there at this time, all political prisoners. As is well known, East Tennessee was loyal to the Union, and old, gray-headed men of all classes — all too old for military service under the law — were arrested for their political faith and confined in this prison. It was reeking with dirt and vermin. Old men sixty-five and seventy years of age were there who had not changed their clothes for three months. They were so crowded in the prison they could hardly all lie down at once on the floor. There were no beds

---

[26] "Sketches of the rise, progress, and decline of secession; with a narrative of personal adventures among the rebels," Also known as "Parson Brownlow's Book", by William Gannaway Brownlow, 1862.

Parson Brownlow entering the Knoxville Jail. (Page 308.)

ENGRAVING SHOWING WILLIAM BROWNLOW BEING CONFINED BY CONFEDERATE AUTHORITIES AT THE KNOXVILLE JAIL, WHICH IS INCLUDED IN "PARSON BROWNLOW'S BOOK."

or provisions of any kind for sleeping, or I saw none, and the only rest I had during the night was lying on a bench I found along the side of a room in the after part of the night. Still I was getting used to hardships and stood it fairly well. I longed for the morning to come; and wondered what the day would bring.

When it did come I could see to examine of the condition of the prison and the kind of prisoners confined there. About eight o'clock the prisoners were marched out and lined up in the yard in front of the building for roll-call and breakfast.

When we were in line with the balance I recognized among the officers present the Provost-Marshal who had sent us to jail the night before. After we had been given our breakfast there was a call for the men from the 58th N.C. to step to the front. We obeyed.

The Captain approached us, greeted us cordially, and took our names. He said he would inform our regiment that we were here, and our Colonel would send for us, and he would then deal with us as he saw fit. "In the meantime," said he, "I will send you out to camp near the city and detain you under guard until your Colonel sends for you."

He then took two dollars from his pocket and handed it to me, saying he would pay us for the fish he got from us the night before.

We were then taken out to camp, at the east edge of the city, put in a tent, and kept under guard about two weeks, and then released, and detailed to do guard duty. The soldiers in the camp were stragglers and those absent from their commands for various reasons. There was no regular command there, and we did all kinds of duty. The fear of punishment had now entirely disappeared, and as the weather was cold and the Winter just setting in, we decided not to try to get away at that time, but to wait and go back to our regiment and stay till Spring, and then make another effort. The reason we felt sure we would not be punished was that we knew our Colonel knew where we were, and had he intended to punish us he would have immediately sent for us, or at least that is the way we reasoned.

We were detailed as teamsters, and gone on a trip to Kingston, about forty miles west of Knoxville, with a wagon-train. The teams were there turned over to another command, and we were ordered back to Knoxville. This was December 22nd, 1862. We took the train, arriving at Knoxville in the afternoon. When we stepped from the train a Sergeant and four men from our company were waiting at the station for us, and ordered us under arrest. Our company had at last sent for us, and we were ready to go. We started at once on foot across the country to join our regiment, which had moved from Tazewell to Big Creek Gap, about fifty miles north of Knoxville. We traveled that evening five or six miles, when night overtook us. We stopped at a farm-house and remained over night.

AGAIN WITH THE REGIMENT

We continued our journey the next day which was the twenty-third, and on the evening of the twenty-fourth we joined our regiment. When we were nearing the camp I asked permission of the officer who had us in charge to allow me to go at once to the Colonel's quarters, to which he readily assented. When we reached his quarters I walked in, saluted him, and said:

"Colonel, we have been absent without leave, and we now report for duty, and beg that you will pardon us for this offense."

He proceeded to give us a lecture as to our duty, said he hoped this would be a lesson for us, and that we would never commit an error like this again, and assured us that if we ever should that we would be punished to the full extent of the law.

"And now," said he, addressing the guard, "you are discharged:" and turning and addressing us, said: "Now, boys, go to your quarters, and be better men in the future." We thought that was getting off pretty easy, and I guess it was.

The boys were all glad to see us, and anxious to know where we had been and how it all had happened. We now settled down to the ordinary routine of camp life, when not on duty trying to pass the time at some kind of amusement, but every day I grew more and more restless and discontented.

It was now Midwinter, and looked like a desperate undertaking in start on a tramp through the mountains at this season of the year. I fully realized the fact that when I started again the 58th N.C. regiment must not and should never get me again. But I was not idle. I was constantly sowing seeds of discontent among the boys, always talking for the Union and against the South, to those whom I could trust, and at least half of the regiment or perhaps more were just as loyal to the Union as those who wore the blue; but they were forced to go to the army, and afraid to try to get away. Poor fellows, how often have I heard them bemoan their unfortunate and unhappy lot, and with tears in their eyes send up a prayer that the Union army would crush the rebellion, and again give them that freedom they once enjoyed under the old flag. I would then say to them: "Go with me, and we will find that freedom."

Often they have said to me: "If I were like you I would go but I have a family — a wife and little children, who will cry for bread. How can I leave them to suffer? It may be the war will end before long, and I can then go home to them."

This was about the kind of conversation that was kept up around the camp fires. I began to grow very impatient, and commenced to plan another effort to escape. Among those who wanted to go with me this time was one who had been with me before, and seven others, whom I had selected, making nine in all.

ANOTHER ATTEMPT TO ESCAPE

They selected me as the leader, and pledged allegiance and loyalty to me under any and all circumstances. So we began perfecting our plans and arrangements. It was now the first of February, the worst month in the year for such an undertaking. We tried to content ourselves and put it off till Spring, but we grew more impatient every day, and at last decided to start. Our plans were all completed, and on the night of February 10, 1863, after taps, when all was asleep save the sentinel on his beat, we hastily gathered up the provisions we had prepared to take with us, slipped from our tents while our comrades slept, and under the cover of darkness passed the guards.[27]

We soon found ourselves in the open country and now commenced one of the most memorable and perilous tramps that I experienced during the period covered by this story.

The night was unusually dark and misting with rain, and the ground soft and muddy. We traveled as rapidly as we could, in order to get as far as possible from the camp before morning. In the after part of the night we traveled the road that led through the country in the direction we thought we wanted to go. At the first gray streaks of the morning we left the road and went into the woods, and when daylight came a heavy fog had settled down on the ground. There was a difference of opinion among us as to the

---

[27] Records show that William H. Younce deserted on February 10, 1863, at Big Creek Gap, Tennessee. Source: North Carolina. Division of Archives and History. North Carolina Troops 1861-1865 A Roster. 14 vols., Raleigh: University Graphics, 1993.

points of the compass. We were from eight to ten miles perhaps from where we had started. We sat down to rest and ate our breakfast and consulted as to the direction we ought to go. After some time we agreed as to the proper course and started, which proved to be right, as we found about the middle of the forenoon by the sun breaking through the clouds.

The ranges of the mountains in that country run parallel, northeast and southwest, with valleys thickly-settled between them. We had reached the mountains east of the valley in which we had been traveling, and we felt perfectly safe. We could follow the summit of those mountains and see all the country up and down the valleys on each side for miles. So in daytime we would follow the summit and at night cross the valley and reach the mountain beyond, often wading creeks above our knees; but we were used to hardships, and really enjoyed the excitement. If we grew tired und wanted to rest, we would lie down on the dry leaves that we would find under the trunks of fallen trees or shelving rocks, and sleep as soundly as though we had been in a warm bed. After we had been out about three days, our provisions give out. We then had to devise some means to get something to eat.

We struck on a plan which proved entirely satisfactory. We would keep a lookout for a house that was pretty well isolated from the neighborhood around it, in the coves or heads of the little valleys along the foot of the mountain We would approach the house as near as we could under cover of the woods. All the boys would conceal themselves except myself and a comrade by the name of Jones.[28] He and I would walk boldly to the house, with the understanding that if they were Union people we would signal the boys to come, and if not we would throw them off their guard by any kind of misrepresentation to suit the occasion, and join the boys after we had passed out of sight of the house. This plan worked all right, for nearly all these poor mountain people in that country were loyal to the Union, and would divide the last crust of bread, for the most of them had sons, brothers or husbands who were conscripts and concealing themselves in the mountains at that time.

Fortunately we were not beggars. We had Confederate money sufficient to pay our way, but these good people would never charge or take anything for their kindness. They would not only furnish us with provisions, but would often go with us and pilot us for miles, directing us around any danger that might be ahead of us.

The worst thing we had to contend with was the weather. It rained a great deal of the time, and frequently was quite cold. Our clothing was scant, and was beginning to get badly worn, especially our shoes.

After we had been out about ten days one of the boys began to complain. He said he believed he would give out. He was one of two brothers that were in the crowd. He dragged himself along for a day or two after he got sick. We all tried to encourage him; told

---

[28] Not surprisingly, there are many soldiers named Jones in Company L. The names I found include: Jesse F., Memock, John, and Jason Jones

him he must not think of giving up, but he continued to grow worse. His pulse became more rapid and his face was flushed with fever. It was sometime in the forenoon, the rain was falling in torrents. In spite of all we could do, he lay down on the cold, wet ground; said he could go no further, and begged that we go on, and let him die alone. He said if we undertook to take care of him, we would all be captured, and for us to leave him and save ourselves. We were at a loss to know what to do. We could not think of leaving him alone. We counseled as to what was the best to do. Of course his brother would not go and leave him to die alone. We gathered a lot of dry leaves and made a bed for him under the trunk of a fallen tree, and gathered bark from trees and covered him to protect him from the rain, and placed him there as gently as we could, and as the tears coursed down their faces we bade the boys good-bye and started on our journey. The young man sat on the log, beside his sick brother's bed, and waved his hand to us as we disappeared around the side of the mountain.

And I have never known what became of these brothers – whether they were captured or died. I have often wished I did know, for I will never forget that sad parting. We had eaten nothing during the day, and after we had left these two comrades we began to look out for something to eat, but it seemed that fate was against us. We found no house that we thought would be safe. Night came on; we crossed the valley east of us, ascended the mountain again, and in the after part of the night, lay down on the ground when we again resumed our journey.

He was left alone with his sick brother.

FROM THE NATIONAL TRIBUNE, DEC 7, 1899

We were aware that Ashby's Confederate cavalry[29] was in camp in the valley east of us. From our position on the mountain we could see their camp.

Our purpose was to get around them. Of course, their presence made us more cautious. We followed the summit of the mountain until about noon, when we saw a house at the head of a little valley on the east side of the mountain, and after taking in the situation, decided we would approach the house for something to eat.

We followed a ridge that ran down nearly to the house, when the boys hid in the underbrush, and Jones and I, as usual, went to the house. We had not been there five minutes when I discovered that we were not among friends. The old lady and daughters were busy cooking dinner over an old-fashioned fireplace, and just as we were shaping our conversation for an excuse to start, two Confederate cavalrymen rode up. They dismounted, threw the reins of their bridles over the gate-posts, and came walking in the house. One of the soldiers was the son of the man who lived there, and the other a comrade of his. They belonged to Ashby's Cavalry, that was camped down in the valley a few miles below, as I have before stated, and the young man had brought his comrade up to his home for dinner. They were armed with the ordinary cavalry sidearms, and while we did not intend that they should arrest us, had they attempted to do so, our policy was not to get into trouble, but by

---

[29] The 7th Virginia Cavalry, formerly led by Col. Turner Ashby, who died in battle in 1862.

some sharp practice of diplomacy or misrepresentation, throw them off their guard so they would not suspect us.

As I usually did the talking, I at once engaged them in conversation. Said I: "We are glad to come up again with our command; have been to our homes over in Kentucky, and just by accident learned our command was down here in the valley."

"What command do you mean?" asked one of them.

"Gen. Marshall's," said I. "We belong to Marshall's Brigade."[30]

"Well," said he, "you are mistaken. Our command — Ashby's Cavalry — is down there, but I know Marshall's Brigade is not, and I do not know where it is."

I expressed great surprise at the information he had given us. By this time dinner was ready, and we were cordially invited to eat dinner with them — and, by the way, it was a very appetizing dinner, especially for one who had not eaten anything for thirty-six hours, — and we very readily accepted the invitation. We continued our conversation. They asked me a great many questions which I answered by guess, presuming they were as ignorant of the make-up of Marshall's Brigade as I was. I knew it had some Kentucky regiments in it, and in answer to their questions I said we belonged to the 12th Kentucky.[31] Our Colonel's name was

---

[30] Humphrey Marshall was a General from Kentucky. He had previously been ambassador to China under president Franklin Pierce.

[31] At the time, there was no 12th Kentucky in the Confederate army. The Confederate 12th Kentucky Cavalry mustered into service in September, 1863 in Mississippi. There were Union 12th Kentucky regiments - the 12th Kentucky Infantry and the 12th Kentucky Cavalry, however.

Campbell; that we were from White County; had left our command up in south-west Virginia; had been home on a furlough, and were now returning.

I watched them carefully to see whether or not I could detect anything from their countenances, but the story seemed answering our purpose, and they were apparently taking it all in.

In due time dinner was over. We arose from the table, and walked out in the yard. One of the young men beckoned to his comrade. They walked some distance from us, and engaged in a low conversation, after which one of them mounted his horse and rode off down the road. This aroused my suspicion, thinking perhaps he had gone to report us, and would return with more soldiers and attempt to capture us. The other young man said, if we desired, he would go with us, and put us on the direct road leading to Rogersville, some six or eight miles down the valley.

I had been to Rogersville before, and that was one of the last places I wanted to go just at this time. I thanked him for his seeming kindness, but said if our command was not down there it would be a trip for nothing, and I could see no need of our going. I suggested to Jones that we turn north and follow the main road into Virginia, where we left our brigade, and we would certainly find it some place up there. I stepped inside the door and asked the old lady our bill, to which she replied:

"Not a cent; not a cent, sir. it shall never be said of me when I am dead and gone that I charged a poor soldier that was fighting for his country for a meal's victuals."

I thanked her for her kindness, and we bade them good-by and started up the road. Soon as we passed out of sight of the house we turned into the woods and joined our companions "A guilty conscience needs no accuser," and we were very doubtful as to whether or not our entertainers had accepted our story. As the country was full of soldiers, we thought it best to at once conceal ourselves.

We ascended the mountain as rapidly as possible. We came to a rugged cliff on the side of the mountain covered with laurel and shrubbery peculiar to that country, — so dense a person could scarcely get through it — and in that thicket we sat down to wait for night, with the intention of then making our escape from that part of the country. But as evening approached, however, the clouds began to gather, and just as darkness began to envelop the mountain, the rain commenced to fall in torrents.

It grew darker and darker until not a ray of light penetrated that dismal gloom. We started to make our way from this hiding place, but found it impossible to make any headway on account of the darkness; besides, we knew we were surrounded by yawning precipices over which we were liable to plunge.

The only thing then left for us to do was to remain there till morning.

A NIGHT OF SUFFERING

I will never forget the agonies and suffering of that night. We sat on the cold rocks, huddled together, trying to keep warm. It rained incessantly until the after part of the night when the wind began to blow and turn cold. We had no way of telling the time, and could only guess as to how the night was passing. We eagerly watched for the first streaks of light over the summit of the mountains in the east. Jones and I were more fortunate than the balance of the men. We had had dinner the day before, while the others had had nothing to eat for nearly two days, and we were all suffering terribly with cold and hunger.

At last the morning dawned, and just as soon as it was light enough to see we started. After a short time we got in the open woods. We counseled as to the best thing to do, and we determined to stop at the first house we came to; that we would all go together, and, let them be friend or foe, we would get something to eat, and that every man would die before he would be captured. With this understanding we began to look for a house. Finally we came to place a short distance from the main road in grove of forest trees. We all went together, We told them we were cold and hungry, and asked them to allow us to warm and dry ourselves and give us something to eat. They received us kindly and invited us in the house.

We had been in the house but a few moments when we found they were good Union people. We told them our story — that we were trying to make our escape from the rebel army. The good woman at once went to work and prepared a splendid breakfast for us, while a good-sized boy stood guard some distance from the house, in order to give an alarm should any soldiers approach. After we had eaten our breakfast and warmed and dried ourselves, we felt very much refreshed. We insisted on paying these good people for their kindness, but they refused to take anything, and when we were ready to start the old man taking each one by the hand, asked God to bless and protect us. The boy went with us five or six miles to pilot us by the safest paths and out of the way of the soldiers that were prowling through the country.

This was on Friday, and we had been out just two weeks. Our purpose was to get to the Holston River that day, and cross it at night. It was a dark, foggy day, and about noon we thought we were in the vicinity of the river. We went down into a dark, deep wood between the hills, built a fire and sat by it all afternoon, waiting for night to come to cross the river.

When night came we started, but found we were yet about four miles from the river, and we found, further, that it was impossible to cross it at night. So we had to wait again for morning. The recent heavy rains had so swollen the river that it was just inside its banks, — a muddy, ugly, turbulent stream — and the only way to cross was to find a canoe or flatboat of which there were many, if we could be fortunate enough to find one anchored on our side. As soon as it was light enough to see we crossed the open bottoms that lay along the river, and started up the stream with the hope of finding a canoe or something on which we could cross. We had traveled two or three miles up the west bank, when, some distance further up, we saw two or three men in a canoe crossing over to the east bank. We hallooed at them, and endeavored to attract their attention, but failed to make them hear. We watched them land on the opposite bank and enter a two-story frame residence that stood nearby. We walked on as rapidly as we could, and about the time we got to the landing the colored man who had gone over with the canoe returned.

A VERY NARROW ESCAPE

We asked him if he would take us over, to which he replied that he would. All the boys got in the canoe except Jones and I. It would not carry us all and the old negro would have to return for us.

While we were waiting for him to return three Confederate cavalrymen rode up, dismounted and hitched their horses. They said they would go over with us.

We all got aboard, the old darky shoved us from the shore, and we started over. The soldiers said they belonged to Gen. Marshall's Brigade, and that their Colonel and Mr. Lyons, who lived on the bank of the river, had just gone over before them, and that Lyons was an enrolling officer.

We had found Marshall's Brigade when we were not looking for it, and the next thing for us to do was to get away from it. Had we made ourselves heard or attracted attention of that Colonel and Lyons, there is no doubt but we would have been captured and killed. The soldiers who crossed with Jones and me treated us quite unsuspectingly, asked if we were going home on furlough; to which we answered in the affirmative. When we landed we were not more than fifty yards from the house which the soldiers entered. Fortunately no one in the house, apparently, saw us.

We started east on the main road, running perhaps a mile before entered a wood along the base of a mountain. We soon reached these woods, when we at once left the road and sought refuge in the mountains. After traveling for some distance, until we

Three Confederate Cavalrymen drove up.

FROM THE NATIONAL TRIBUNE, DEC 14, 1899

felt perfectly safe, we sat down to rest and recount the scenes and dangers of the morning. We fully realized that we had run a great risk, and had a very narrow escape.

This was on Saturday, February 25, and it began to rain in the afternoon. We had nothing to eat during the day, and were very hungry, as well as tired, but we traveled on till about night, when we came to a log cabin beside the little road we were following.

We believed it would be safe to remain over night if the family who lived there were Union people, and we felt sure they were. We enter the house all together, told them we were wet and hungry, wanted something to eat, and to remain with them over night. They very kindly took us in, prepared supper for us, and the old gentleman built a fire out of logs in an old-fashioned fireplace. We found them, as we had expected, good Union people. After we had eaten our supper, the old man assured us we were perfectly safe, and they spread a lot of quilts and comforts on the floor in front of the fire for us to lie on. I am sure I never slept sounder or rested better in all my life than I did that night.

We arose next morning quite early, in order to have breakfast prepared by daylight. Our clothes had dried, and we felt very much refreshed. After breakfast the old gentleman instructed us as to the best and safest route, and we again resumed our journey.

Turning east we left the regular range of mountains, and had twenty or twenty-five miles of open country to travel over. Taking advantage of the by-paths, and leaping in the woods as much as possible, we traveled all day and made good progress. About dark we had reached Jonesboro, which we passed on the north, keeping at a distance of a half a mile or more from the town. After we reached the railroad, north of the town, we started up the track, and had gone but a short distance, when we entered a deep cut. Just then we heard a train coming toward us. Fortunately the bank was not so steep but we could climb it, which we did on double-quick time, and were just on the top of the bank when the train sped by.

We traveled on till, perhaps, ten o'clock at night, when we reached a wood. We were tired and almost worn out, and decided to lie down and sleep. It was quite cold, and the ground was freezing, but we lay as close together as we could and slept till morning.

When daylight came, and we were ready again to start, for the second time during our trip we had lost the points of the compass. It was cloudy and foggy, and we could not see any distance. After considerable argument, for we did not agree, we started and traveled two or three miles, when we all agreed that we were wrong; we turned and retraced our steps, and some time in the forenoon the sun broke through the clouds and we found that we were right.

We made but little progress that day. The country was full of Confederate cavalry, and we had to play hide and seek with them all day around the hills and knobs. At one time we were close enough to a squad of them to have tossed a stone down among them from our position on the hillside above the road where we were concealed. We were scarcely out of sight of them during the larger part of the day, but I am sure not a single one of them saw us. Late in the evening, about sunset, we reached the base of the mountain, and we welcomed it as place of safety.

We stopped at a cabin and found them to be Union people. They gave us our supper, which we appreciated very much, for we had had nothing to eat during the day. We also rested and slept there till the after part of the night, when one of the men who lived there, and was also a conscript and scouting, went with us some distance to pilot us around danger that was just ahead of us.

We crossed the mountain in the morning about daylight, and by eight o'clock we were in Doe River Cove, in Carter County, Tenn., a section of country noted for all living there being Union people. We then felt safe, for we knew we were then among friends. We traveled the main road and by noon came to the neighborhood where I had been the August before with the old Baptist preacher before referred to in this story.

At the earnest solicitation of these good people, with whom we stopped, we remained till the following morning.

On Wednesday morning we again resumed our journey, and by noon we had reached Doe Mountain, starting northeast at Watauga River, which runs eighteen or twenty miles, when it terminates abruptly at Mountain City, in Johnson County.

We at once ascended the mountain, followed its summit, and as we had done before, when night settled down upon us we made beds of leaves, and lay down and slept till morning. We reached the terminus of the mountain at Mountain City that evening about dark. The rain was again falling in torrents.

AT HOME AGAIN

Our purpose was to try to reach my father's home that night, but about the middle of the night we had given out with fatigue and hunger, and could go no further. We stopped at a cabin with people whom I knew, and lay down on the floor and slept till nearly daylight, and then started for home. We arrived at my father's home about eight o'clock in the morning, on Friday, the third day of March, having been on the road just three weeks to a day.

The boys who were with me went to their homes in another part of the County, and thus ended my second desertion.

I will not attempt to describe the condition of things that existed there at that time. My vocabulary is too limited to attempt a portrayal of the horrors and the sufferings of those poor Union people. Civil law and courts of justice had been abolished; monarchy and ruin reigned supreme; men and neighbors, who had always passed for good men, and who had turned to be rebels, were transformed into demons, murderers and savages. Conscripts were hunted like wild animals, and often shot and murdered. Their homes were often destroyed by the torch, and if spared were robbed of everything they had, and their families left without a crust of bread.

The fact that I had deserted the second time was known by the authorities at home before I arrived. My Captain had instructed the Colonel of the Home Guard, as they called themselves, not to return me again to his company; in fact, not to arrest me, but shoot me on sight, and they were on the lookout for me before I arrived. I

Father informed me I was to be shot on sight.

FROM THE NATIONAL TRIBUNE, DEC 21, 1899

was informed of these facts as soon as I got home. I then doubled my vigilance, for I well knew with me then it was simply a matter of life or death. I decided to find a hiding-place and allow no one to see me, and at night I would slip in and get something to eat. Every two or three nights five or six of them would come and search the house from cellar to garret. But I was very careful not to be there. This was a hard life, and I soon began to grow tired, and at night, as I would lie in my hiding-place in the gloomy forest, I would wonder if there were not some way out of this kind of existence, when just at this time a circumstance occurred in the neighborhood that changed the whole course of things, and opened again new fields for adventure.

There lived not far away an old man by the name of Price.[32] He had four or five sons who were conscripts, but up to this time had never been captured. The old man had also gained the enmity of these bandits or Home Guards, and they were seeking to capture him. They had camped on his place during a part of the Winter, and robbed him of everything he had. His family had left their home and sought refuge elsewhere. He had an old mill on a mountain stream near his house, and he and his sons would slip in from the mountains and grind corn for bread, and take it back with them to their hiding-place.

---

[32] Jesse Price. The 1860 census lists Jesse, wife Nancy, and children Letridge, Zachariah, Moses, Timothy, and Mary, living near the Younces.

UNION MEN MURDERED

The Home Guards learning they were making frequent visits to the mill, concealed themselves near by, and waited for their coming. Price, thinking the way was clear, with two of his sons and a nephew, came to the mill. They were surrounded, taken by surprise, and all of them captured and taken at once to the County-seat and locked up. The next morning a mob, led by Major Long (the same Major Long who captured me, before referred to) went to the jail, took these prisoners to a wood near the town, and hanged every one of them. They would tie one of the poor fellows' hands behind him, put a rope around his neck, place him on a horse behind one of the mob, who would ride under the limb of the tree, throw the end of the rope to a man on the limb, who would tie it, and the man on the horse would ride out from under him, leaving him dangling in mid-air.

The three boys were hung first, one at a time, as I have described. In the crowd that went out to witness the hanging was a Dr. Wagg,[33] prominent physician, and also a Methodist preacher, a man well and favorably known throughout all that country, and, be it to his credit, was trying to quell the mob and save the lives of these men. After the three young men had been hanged, Dr. Wagg approached the old man, whom he had known for many years, and told him he could do nothing for him; that he had no influence with these men, and they were going to hang him. "And now," he said,

---

[33] Rev. Dr. James Wagg (1808-1881).

"you are unprepared, and in a few minutes more your soul will be ushered into eternity. I am here to try to do you good. Shall I not stay the hand of death, while I pray with you?"

The old man replied:

"Doctor, I have done nothing to be hung for. I am old — not even subject to military duty. I have committed no crime. I have only been loyal to my country, and if it is for this you intend to murder me, I will go into eternity as I am. I want no rebel, such as you are to pray for me."

In a moment his hands were pinioned, and he was swinging beside the three boys.[34]

When they were taken down Dr. Wagg discovered that one of the young men was not yet dead, and after some time spent in working with him, he was resuscitated. He was taken back to jail,

---

[34] This account from the (Confederate-aligned) Fayetteville Weekly Observer, 27 April 1863:

Bushwhackers Hung
For many months past, the mountains along the borders of East Tennessee and North Carolina, in the counties of Johnson and Ashe; have been infested by a band of bushwhackers, led and controlled by one Jesse Price and his sons, who have committed many acts both of murder and robbery. This man Price lived upon Big Rye Cove Ridge, Ashe County, North Carolina. The militia of that county having been called out for his detection and apprehension; he had kept close about home on the lookout for a week or two. Whilst thu [sic] watching in the direction of Jefferson, a company from Grayson, Va., came in upon him from the rear last week, and nabbed him and four of his sons. They were taken to Jefferson, and on Friday last, the old man and three of his sons Hiram, James and Moses were hung, without judge or jury, or benefit of clergy. The fourth son, in consideration of his youth, and the promise that he would discover the hiding places of others of the band, was, after the rope had been tied around his neck, permitted to live.

and as soon as he was fully recovered was sent to the front at Richmond.

He at once made his escape, got to the Union army, and enlisted in the Federal service, and fought throughout the war. [35]

---

[35] Moses became known as "Scape-Gallows" Price, and after escaping, joined the West Virginia infantry.

IN THE MOUNTAINS OF TENNESSEE

This happened about two weeks after my arrival home, and convinced me that it was exceedingly hazardous for me to remain in that part of the country. After due consideration we decided that I should go to Tennessee. I had many friends and acquaintances over there among the Union people, and would be much safer; besides, if I should be so unfortunate as to be captured I perhaps would not be assassinated, but have a chance for my life. With this understanding I completed my arrangements to go, and on a beautiful starlit night, when all nature was hushed in silence, I cautiously crept from my hiding-place, approached the old home, following the little path that led down by the barn and through the back yard up to the house. Father and mother had not yet retired, for they knew I would be there to say good-by. They said they had almost despaired of me ever escaping, and saw no way that I could prevent being murdered by these mid-night murderers. Further, they had just learned that day that there had been a reward offered for me, dead or alive. I tried to encourage them and comfort them all I could.

Said I: "You look upon the dark side only. You must remember there is another side to this question. I know it looks dark for me now, but I believe I will some day get away from these accursed rebels, and again breathe the air of freedom; and in order that I may reach my destination as soon as possible tomorrow, and get beyond the limit of my own State before morning, I will say good-by."

Turning, I hurried down the path, and was soon in the woods, lost in the shadow of the hills. I followed the path through the woods along the summit of the hills that I had now become familiar with. I sped along quite rapidly, and crossed the State line about daylight. When I began to descend the west side of the Allegheny Mountains I traveled more leisurely, occasionally sitting down to rest.

It was sometime in the afternoon when I reached the home of my friends where I expected to stop. There were many young men who were conscripted and scouting, and I was welcomed among them, None of them had ever been captured, and they would sit for hours and eagerly listen to the story of my experience, of my capture, desertion, imprisonment and suffering in my final escape from my regiment.

I tried to content myself with these boys, for I felt comparatively secure, but in a few days I grew restless, and discontented. Life in the dismal gloom of these old mountains grew more and more monotonous. I so expressed myself to my companions. They said: "We will try to stand it this Summer, and by Fall the Union army will be in reach of us, and we will then make a break for freedom."

I said: "I cannot stand this till Fall. I am actually forced to seek a different life. If I should try to stay here I would expose myself in some way, so that I would be captured, and that means more to me than to either of you, Besides, I cannot live secluded from the world, as we are now doing. To continue this would drive me insane."

IN DIFFICULTY AGAIN

Just at this time we learned that there had arrived in the neighborhood a young Confederate officer from Virginia, who was recruiting for the artillery service. The idea at once struck me that I would see him, state my case — simply tell him the whole story — and if he could, under those circumstances, accept me in his company, take me from that country, and protect me from my old regiment, I would enlist and go with him, and as soon is we would get in reach of the Union army, I would make my escape into the lines. I expressed my purpose to my companions. They vigorously protested against it, did all they could to induce me to remain; but my mind was made up to get out of those mountains, and away from the dangers that surrounded me there. I at once addressed a note to this young officer, whose name was Oliver,[36] and sent it by a friend, stating that on the next day at a certain hour I would be glad to meet him at a certain place, provided he would come under a truce, unarmed and alone.

He answered by a messenger, saying he had heard of me; would meet me, and would comply with all the conditions mentioned, and would expect me to do the same. As he was a total stranger, and stated he had heard of me, I felt a little nervous, for fear he might take advantage of his opportunity and capture me: and then, again, I thought that if he was a Captain of artillery, he

---

[36] Captain John Mayo Oliver, Company K, 21st Virginia Cavalry. The unit began as artillery, but was transferred to the cavalry service after the battle at Wytheville, Virginia.

would not violate his word under a truce. So on the next day, when the hour came, we met in the woods at the place agreed upon, and I got myself into more trouble.

We arrived almost at the same time. He greeted me cordially and expressed himself as pleased to meet me. He was a young man of fine address, about four or five yours my senior. He wore an artillery uniform with the rank of Captain. We sat down on a log and began to talk of the war and the condition of the country. Said his battery was doing garrison duty, and was not at the front; that he had eight or ten recruits, and in a day or two would start to his command. "And, by the way," said he, "I understand you are a deserter; have deserted twice, and the authorities over in your State have offered a reward for your capture; and, further that if they got you, they will not send you back to your regiment, but will make an example of you, as a warning to others."

"Captain," said I, "your information is correct. I have deserted twice from the 58th North Carolina, and I have understood the local authorities over in my State intend to kill me if they can get sight of me. Do you know whether or not this is actually their intention?"

"Yes." said he, "I know of my own knowledge it is a fact, and there is but one way of safety for you, and that is to get out of this country. Your regiment does not want you, and will never look for you, and I will make this suggestion: that you enlist and go with me, I will accept you as a conscript, muster you into the service again, and I will guarantee that you will never be disturbed."

"Captain," said I, "that is just what I am thinking of doing, provided that you will guarantee to protect me from punishment for anything that has happened in the past."

Clasping my hand he said: "I pledge you my honor that I will use every means in my power to protect you, and I assure you, you shall never be disturbed while in my company; and, further, there is a vacancy in my company, and I will appoint you Second Sergeant, and put you in line for promotion. The reason I do this is that a man who has suffered for his own errors, as you have, I believe will yet make a good soldier."

Well, to make a long story short, we fixed the matter up, and we were to start the next day with the recruits he had. I returned to my companions, told them what I had done, but did not advise a single one to go with me. I remained over night with them, and next morning said good-by.

I found the Captain and recruits at the place designated, ready to start, and in two days we were with the company at New River Bridge, Va., on the line of railroad which is now the Norfolk & Western,[37] where the town of Radford has since been built. We were camped on a bluff overlooking the railroad bridge that spanned the river. We were in a fort, with six pieces of artillery, guarding the bridge.

This was the first of April, 1863. We had but little to do, and life again began to grow monotonous; but fortunately in a short

---

[37] In 1982, the Norfolk and Western Railway merged with the Southern Railway to form Norfolk Southern Corporation.

time we were ordered to Dublin, a short distance west, and our Captain was appointed Provost Marshall, and the company did provost guard duty.[38] I was detailed to duty on the railroad, making alternately a 24-hour run. We were allowed two men as guards with us on the train. We were under martial law, and it was my duty to see that every passenger had a proper pass. I would go on duty at eight o'clock in the morning, and it was supposed that the train was turned over to me properly worked by the Sergeant whom I relieved, and that I would turn it back to him the same way next morning.

I liked this work very well, for the reason that it was a change from the ordinary army life; and another reason, it was a good train for deserters when I had it, and many a poor fellow I helped along. I was expected to arrest every deserter, or any one else who did not have the right kind of a pass; but there was no danger of me arresting any one, when I had been a deserter twice myself.

During all the time I did duty on the road I never made a single arrest.

---

[38] The Provost Marshall is the head of the Military Police, and Provost Guard Duty is equivalent to Military Police duty.

AIDING A DESERTER

There was one circumstance that happened one day that is worth reading. I had gone on duty in the morning at the usual time, had made the run east, and met the train coming out from Lynchburg. As soon as I changed cars with the guard and got aboard the west-bound train the conductor said to me that a deserter was on the train, and the officer I had relieved had failed to arrest him. He said he would show him to me. I started through the train with him; and when we stepped into the car where he was, he pointed him out to me. He wore the uniform of a cavalry Major, and I knew I would have to do something to satisfy the conductor, or he might report me and spoil my job. I said to the conductor that I would examine his pass, and ascertain whether or not he was all right; but the conductor was onto him and said: "I know he is a deserter, and it is your duty to order him under arrest at once."

Knowing that he had no authority over me, and that I ranked him even in the management of the train, I said: "Sir, I understand my duty, without any instructions from you, and will do it as I see fit."

Leaving him I walked down the aisle of the car, approached the officer, and pleasantly asked him for his pass. He looked at me a moment and said: "What authority, sir, have you to ask a commissioned officer for his pass?"

I replied, "I have the authority of General Jones,[39] commanding this department," and at the same time took from my pocket my commission and handed it to him. After examining it he said: "Your authority is good," and handed me his pass.

"How is it," said I, "that you are traveling on a citizen's pass?"

Said he: "I belong to the 10th Texas cavalry; am a prisoner on parole, and am a citizen until I am exchanged."

"You wear the insignia of your rank," said I.

"If that star offends any one," said he, "I will take it off," and taking off his hat pulled off the star that held up one side of the brim.

All this time the conductor was standing in the front of the car watching me. I knew the Major was a deserter, but I did not intend to arrest him, even at the risk of being reported by the conductor.

I walked back to where the conductor was standing, and said to him I was not sure he was a deserter, and that I would remain in the car and watch him; which I did, and when the engineer signaled for the next station he began to gather up his baggage, and soon as the train stopped he got off. I watched him go down the steps and on the platform of the depot, and was much afraid the conductor would see him; but he did not. The train started. I let it get under fairly good headway, when I signaled the engineer to stop, and at the same time started hurriedly through the train. I met the conductor hurrying back, and as soon as he saw me, asked: —

[39] Major General Samuel Jones, commander of the Department of Western Virginia.

"What is the trouble?" I answered him by asking: "What is the matter with the engineer? He has failed to obey orders, and refused to stop the train when signaled to do so, and the Major jumped from the train just as we left the station, and is gone."

He was quite angry, or pretended to be; said he would report me when we got in from our run. I defied him to do it, and told him when it came to that I would have some things to report myself. I was running a bluff on him, for I was really afraid he would report me; but he never did and I never heard of this circumstance again.

By this time I had become partially reconciled and must say was enjoying my work very well. I was clothed with a great deal of authority for one so young, and had gained the perfect confidence of my superiors; and while I was not doing the work assigned me, they did not know it. I was the only one on the train with authority to make an arrest, and if I found a poor fellow whose papers were not right, I simply passed him, just the same, and no one knew anything about it. My Captain, who was a perfect gentleman, always treated me with kindness and consideration, and when I was not on duty much of our time was spent together, and I had almost made up my mind that if I was allowed to remain in this work I would stay, for I knew I was of service to some poor fellow almost every day by passing him and giving him a chance to get away. But while I was thus congratulating myself on my good fortune, a circumstance again occurred that changed the whole course of things.

ADVANCE OF UNION FORCES

On the morning of the 18th of July I went on duty as usual, made the run east, meeting the train from Lynchburg, and returning. When we arrived at Dublin, where our company was, at noon, I found everybody wild with excitement. Our Captain had received a telegram to the effect that the "Yankees" were advancing on Wytheville,[40] about forty miles west of us, and also orders to sidetrack the passenger train, attach flat cars sufficient for our battery and company, and run out to Wytheville as quickly as possible. You can imagine the excitement an order of that kind would create, especially among women, and nearly all our passengers were women, with a few children and old men. We did as ordered — switched the passenger cars, and told the passengers they would have to remain there until an engine could reach them from the other end of the road.

We coupled on two flat cars, loaded two six-pound guns and two caissons, and hitched on a passenger car behind for the company, and when we were all aboard ordered the engineer to pull the throttle wide open, and we thought he did, judging from the speed he attained.[41] We were all in good spirits, and felt that we

---

[40] The Battle of Wytheville, also known as Toland's Raid, fought 18 July 1863.

[41] General Jones' report stated he sent a newly created unit of 130 men and 2 artillery pieces to Wytheville via an impressed passenger train.

Source: Scott, Robert N. (1889). The War of the Rebellion: a Compilation of the Official Records of the Union and Confederate Armies Series I Volume XXVIII Part II. Washington, DC: Government Printing Office. OCLC 318422190.

were just going out on a pleasant trip. We believed it was a false alarm. We were then perhaps one hundred miles from the Federal lines, and I believed it impossible for an army of Union soldiers to be in that part of the country. Our conduct on the train that evening was more like that of a crowd of young people going to a picnic than to a battle. We were all enjoying ourselves and fully expected to return to camp that night.

The train pulled up to the station at Wytheville two hours before sunset, and we were then convinced that we were mistaken in our opinion. The Union soldiers were reported within four miles of town, and advancing. There were perhaps 2,000 Confederate soldiers there, but no regular command. I saw and realized that I was again in a trap: for, as I have said before, I had registered a vow in heaven that I would never fire a gun against my country's flag, and here I was ready to go into a fight, and I saw no way of escape.

There was a detail made from the company to man the two pieces of artillery. We had to be commanded by the Captain and Second Lieutenant, and the balance of the company was given muskets and assigned to the infantry, commanded by the First Lieutenant. I being the ranking Sergeant with the infantry, my place was at the head of the company, and it can readily be seen that placed me in a very responsible position. I will not attempt here to describe the scenes that were now taking place. Only those who have witnessed the excitement on the eve of battle are able to fully appreciate the awfulness of the situation. Couriers, whose horses are white with foam, dashing in every direction, the shrill and exciting command of officers, the rattling of sabers, the blanched cheek of the soldier, make a scene that will never be forgotten by those who have witnessed it.

Our orders were to march double-quick north through the town, and attack the Federal cavalry as they advanced. As we passed through the town women were running in all directions, some of them with children, trying to seek some place of safety. All the business houses were locked and deserted. Going north from the town there was a slight elevation extending perhaps a half mile or more to the summit, and when our advance reached there the Federal cavalry was in line but a short distance beyond quietly waiting for the attack. Quickly the order came down the line to fall back to the town and at the same time a regular stampede commenced in front. Our company double-quicked back to town, and at the same time the Federals ordered a cavalry charge. As soon as they reached the summit they opened fire and poured a continuous volley into our men. The Confederates were now in utter rout and confusion. Lieutenant Humes[42] rallied our company, and we formed on a corner of a street, on the sidewalk, but not a man fired a gun, though our Lieutenant marched up and down in front of the company with drawn sword, ordering the men to load and fire.

---

[42] Frank A. and Andrew R. Humes were both Lieutenants in Company K.

THE ADVENTURES OF A CONSCRIPT

CHARGED BY CAVALRY

The cavalry was coming, as fast as their horses could run, and I knew we could stay there but a moment until they would be upon us. I was getting extremely anxious for the boys to break ranks and run, when our Lieutenant gave the command to break ranks and save ourselves. You can be assured this order was quickly obeyed. The cavalry was less than two squares from us. We started up the street and came to a stairway leading up into a three-story block, but closed and locked by folding doors. A big fellow just in front of me struck the lock with the breech of his gun and the door flew open. About fifteen of our company got up that stairway and more would have got in had not the cavalry been so close to them. We followed the stairway until we reached the third floor, and stopped in a picture gallery, but found no one in, and I hardly think anyone wanted his picture taken, even if the photographer had been there. The first thing we did was to stack arms and get ready to surrender, thinking there was no way of escape, and that they would be sure to get us. From our elevated position we could see everything that was going on in and around the town. The Confederates never rallied, and were chased in every direction like rabbits. It really looked like sport for the Federal soldiers. They would gallop across the fields toward clump of woods or thicket, and as they would approach them the Confederates would jump out and take to their heels. They would fire a few shots after them and turn and ride back. While we were interested in these scenes we heard footsteps ascending the stairway. We bunched ourselves together,

Main Street, Wytheville, as it appeared around the time of the Civil War.

ready to surrender. We could hear the footsteps approaching nearer and nearer, when suddenly the door was thrown open by an officer with pistol in his hand, and two or three of the boys exclaimed: "We surrender!"

They had been too hasty, for the officer was none other than our own Major. He replied "You cowardly rascals, what are you doing up here. Get your guns and come down; we have them nearly whipped." The question occurred to me what he was doing up there. No one paid any attention to his order; but he left, and I presume hid in some other part of the building.

I must not forget to speak of the part our two pieces of artillery played in this fight. They followed immediately in rear of the infantry, and just as the Union cavalry reached the main street of the town in their wild charge, one piece commanded by the Second Lieutenant had unlimbered and fired one shot, when it was captured, and just at this time Captain Oliver and the Orderly-Sergeant came dashing up the streets seated on their gun, the drivers having jumped from their horses and turned them loose. They came dashing around the corner at a fearful speed, and plunged right through the first line of Union cavalry and had got a square or more further on, when two of the horses were shot down, and as the soldiers gathered around, Captain Oliver, mounting to his feet on the gun and swinging his sword above his head, said he would surrender to no man but his equal, meaning a commissioned officer. Finally an officer, seeing the confusion, spurred his horse through the crowd, and when in reach the Captain handed him the hilt of his sword. They then started to the rear with him and the Sergeant, and when they had walked about a square, Captain Oliver was struck near the heart by a Minié ball and fell to the ground dead. He exclaimed, "I am killed," and addressing the Orderly-Sergeant said: "Take this ring from my finger and send it to my sister and my watch send it to my mother," and those were his last words. The guard allowed the Sergeant to stop and take the ring and watch, and then left him dead on the sidewalk. His body was next day taken up from the street, the Orderly-Sergeant was paroled, and he took the body home to his friends, near Richmond, for burial, and delivered the ring and watch as his dying words directed.[43] I was shocked at the news of his death, for though differing with him on the issue of the war, I admired him for his manliness, integrity, courage and loyalty, even though in a bad cause. I felt that a young man with bright and promising life for future usefulness was gone, and that I had lost a good and faithful friend.

I will now return to the story of myself and those with me in the third floor of the brick block on the main street of the town. We remained up there until between sunset and dark when some women in the block, who knew we were up there, came up a back stairway and said the town had been set on fire on the opposite side of the street, and it was not safe for us to remain as the block we were in was likely to be set on fire from the burning buildings. Every street in the town was a surging mass of Union soldiers, and everything was simply at their mercy. So, following the directions of these women, we hastily slipped our shoes from our feet, so as to make no noise. We then followed them, as they led the way down a back stairway, landing us in the alley, and when we had reached the ground they directed us some distance further back to a

---

[43] General Jones' report lists Oliver and two privates as the only Confederate dead from the battle. Oliver was buried in a family cemetery in Mecklenburg County, Virginia.

lot that had been planted with corn, and perhaps a hundred and fifty feet square. The corn was taller than our heads, making a good hiding place.

We lay flat down on the ground between the rows of corn, and although the Union soldiers passed in great crowds along the street within an hundred feet of us, I felt comparatively safe. I got a little nervous at one time. A stable stood on the corner of the lot, and about ten o'clock a crowd of them came and broke down the door and got a horse that had been locked in. It took them a long time to break the door, or at least we thought so, and the blaze of the burning building made it as light as day. I was afraid they would have some occasion to pass through the lot, and I knew if they did they would fall over some of us. They thoroughly sacked and burned a part of the town, and about eleven o'clock we heard the bugle signal to fall in line, and in a short time they had started on their march back over the same road they had come, and by midnight the town was as still as the grave, not a sound broke the dead silence, save now and then the rattling of the horses' feet, of some straggler who had failed to join his command, or the muffled footsteps of citizens or soldiers as they slipped from their hiding places to view the fearful ruin that had been wrought.

About this time we slipped from our hiding place and started for the country. We had enough of that kind of town life. When we started we very naturally scattered. Myself and three others remained together.

The reader will ask why I did not go to the Union army, I will answer, for two reasons: First, on account of my ignorance of the usages of war; I fully believed if I should go to them under those circumstances that they would take me a prisoner, send me North, incarcerate me in prison, and exchange and send me back; and second, they were perhaps one hundred and fifty miles outside the Union lines, and with little hope of getting back themselves, and I was, under the circumstances, afraid to fall into their hands, not knowing what kind of treatment I might receive. I feared that my word would not be taken as to my loyalty to the Union when I was caught bearing arms for the South.

THE ADVENTURES OF A CONSCRIPT

AFTER THE BATTLE

To return to my story, we traveled til about three o'clock in the morning, when we came to a large farmhouse not more than four or five miles from the town. The people were all up; the women of the house, for there were no men there, invited us in and of course were eager to hear the news. I told them that the Yankees had burned Wytheville to the ground, torn up the railroad for miles, and our whole regiment was either captured or killed. So far as we know we were the only ones that escaped, and the whole country was full of Yankees, burning, murdering and destroying everything in their course.

They were frightened almost to death, and could hardly refrain from shedding tears of sympathy for us. They offered to prepare us something to eat, which we gladly accepted, and after they had given us an elegant breakfast they sent a boy to conduct us into the hills, where their men folks had their horses concealed and were hiding, themselves. We told them the same story we had told the women. They said we were welcome to remain with them until the Yankees left that part of the country. We sat around and began to get drowsy, having slept none the night before.

We suggested that we would go for some fresh water and walk around a little; we would then perhaps feet better. They gave us their bucket and directed us the way to a spring some distance around the side of the mountain. We told them we would return soon, but after we left them we counseled as to what we would do, and we agreed not to go back, but go on home, which was only forty or fifty miles away, and then go on to the Union army at Knoxville, Tennessee.

We threw their buckets over a precipice and started on our tramp. The story we told these people served us well for a day and a half. We told them our regiment was at Saltville, some distance on the road in the direction we were going; that our battery had been sent to Wytheville: it was captured, and all the company killed and captured except us.

Every time we would tell this story, which was fifty times a day, they would express great sympathy for us, and they gave us the best to eat the country afforded. Before we left the main road and turned in another direction, where I had to invent a new story, I had told the old one so long and so often that I began to believe it myself, and as I would tell of all our company being killed and captured, I could hardly keep back the tears, and that of course helped me to win the sympathy of every one with whom we came in contact.

On the morning of the third day after we started we arrived in the neighborhood of our homes, but we took the precaution to stop in Tennessee. I stopped with the same friends whom I had left the April before. They were glad to have me among them, and were again much interested in the story of my adventures. I only ventured to go to my father's house at night.

I was determined that the authorities there should never get me. I was still about two hundred miles from the Union army; but just at this time Gen. Burnside[44] was advancing up the line of railroad from Knoxville toward the Virginian line, and I felt sure in a month or two I would have no trouble to get to the Union army.

About this time I learned that my Captain had been killed in the fight at Wytheville, and that thirty-seven of the company had deserted; that our company had been transferred to the cavalry service, and was then only about thirty-five or forty miles from my home. So, after taking in the situation, I at once decided to go back to my company and wait there for the nearer approach of the Union army. I believed this to be the safest course for me to pursue. So, slipping to my father's home at night, as I had done before, I again stated my purposes.

Said I, "I will go back to my company, help the Lieutenant reorganize and fill it up, if possible to do so, and when the Union army is close enough, so that I will not have so far to go, I will again desert, come by home, and go on to the Union lines. In from three to six weeks you may expect me back."

---

[44] General Ambrose Burnside, Union General (and the namesake of sideburns).

WITH THE COMPANY AGAIN

So on the first of August, I left again for my company, arriving on the next evening. My Lieutenant was glad to see me back. We talked over the situation and of the probability of our company organization being disbanded. He begged me to assist him in every way I could to recruit the company; said there were but thirty-five or forty men left. I told him I had come to help fill our ranks, so as to maintain our organization, and when that was done of course I expected to be rewarded with a commission, to which he gladly assented. My purpose in making this statement to him was to win his confidence. I had an object in view, and thought he could be of service to me, and perhaps save me trouble; and I can say that I succeeded admirably in worming into his good graces, and in a short time he would have done anything for me that I would ask of him.

Through the month of August we lay in camp with nothing to do. Now and then one of the boys who had deserted would come straggling in, and frequently bring a recruit with him. No one was punished for deserting. They were too glad to get them back to think of punishing them. That was the reason I went back. I knew I would not be punished, and that I was safe then, and scouting in the mountains was not only extremely hazardous, but the most miserable life any one could be subjected to. In fact, I never could scout. I was not cautious enough, but was constantly exposing myself to danger. Though, I knew men personally that lay in those mountains during the three years of the war after they were conscripted, and were never captured; but they had to lie in the mountains like wild animals, their beard and hair grew down over their shoulders, and they were really like wild men.

We were having quite an easy time in camp. We had no duty to do, not even guard duty. Every day I was watching the movements of the Union army. It was steadily advancing, and the Confederates immediately in front of it falling back. About the first day of September it was reported that in a day or two we would draw horses and receive marching orders. I watched every movement carefully, and at last I thought it was time for me to act. On the morning of September 6, 1863, a day that will ever be memorable with me, I went into Lieutenant Humes' tent and began to talk to him about the reorganization of the company; told him I thought we ought to make an effort to get some more men and recruit the company up to seventy-five at least. He agreed with me, but said: "Where can we get them?"

I said to him: "Lieutenant, I have an idea that I desire to submit to you for your consideration, and if it should meet your approval we can try it; and if not, there will be no harm done."

"I am willing," said he, "to hear any suggestion you may wish to make."

"Then," said I, "Lieutenant, you know the mountains along the State line between North Carolina and Tennessee in the vicinity of my home are full of conscripts who have never been in the army, and you know further that you could never find one of them in a year's hunt; but these men are not afraid of me, and I could go into a crowd of twenty-five of them in an hour after I would get there. I was with these men, sleeping with them in the woods, a month ago. They expressed themselves as being very tired of that kind of life, and some of them said to me that they were very much tempted to come with me and join our company, and had I encouraged them I really believe several of them would have come. Now what I want to suggest is that you give me a leave of absence, say, for a week or ten days, with authority to recruit, and I will go over among those men and I will guarantee to bring back not less than fifteen, or more, who will enlist in our company."

After talking and thinking over the matter for some time, he said: "I believe your suggestion is a good one, and there is but one thing in the way, and that is, will you come back?"

Said I: "Lieutenant, I know my record as a soldier is bad, and I have suffered a great deal as you well know, on account of it; but my voluntary return a month ago should be sufficient evidence to you that I am trying to retrieve that which by my own conduct I have lost. But if my pledge of honor is not sufficient, you need not act on my suggestion. It is your commission that is in danger, and not mine, for I never had one, but have the promise of one now, and I believe this to be the proper thing for me to do to get it."

After further conversation, he said: "We will go to the Colonel, and talk to him about it."

We walked down to the Colonel's quarters, and the Lieutenant at once stated the proposition. The Colonel said: "Who is this man you are sending on so important a mission as that? Is he a man you can trust?"

To which the Lieutenant answered: "Colonel, if I can not trust him, I can not trust any man in my company."

The Colonel, without further remarks, picked up his pen and wrote me a leave of absence for eight days on recruiting service. I thanked him, and stated that I felt sure I would do good work, and be able to return with fifteen or twenty men,

I was feeling in good spirits, and felt that I had scored a great victory.

Bidding the Colonel good-bye, we walked back to our company quarters. It was then about nine o'clock in the forenoon, I wanted to start as soon as possible, and I hastily began making preparations to leave. It had got noised through the camp that I was going away, and the boys gathered around to say good-by, little thinking they would never see me back again, but I knew they would not. Many of them were as loyal to the Union as I. I had not communicated my plans to a single one of them; but we had been together so long an attachment had grown up between us, and it was with a feeling of sadness that I took each one of them by the hand. Lieutenant Humes included, and turned my back upon them for the last time. I had made up my mind as to my future course. I believed that the time of my deliverance had come. The leave of absence I had was good any place except in my own County, where I was known; but my purpose was not to let the authorities in my County know I was there, if it were possible to keep it from them. The next evening, after I left camp, I was in the neighborhood of my home. I at once sought the men and friends whom I had come to see. I told them how I came to be there, and asked them how many were ready to go with me to the Union army. I said to them: "Leave this kind of a life; get out of these mountains. The way of escape is now possible, and if we fail to take advantage of this opportunity we deserve to still continue to suffer."

PLANNING TO REACH THE UNION LINES

Some of them agreed with me and some did not, but as soon as one would come on my side he would help me in my work, and it was but a few days until there were twenty-five of them just as enthusiastic as I was. We made our headquarters in Johnson County, Tennessee. There were but few southern sympathizers in the County, and no soldiers, and we felt secure, although we would make no show of ourselves in daytime, but would do all our moving around at night. When we had got all the recruits we thought it possible to get, we began to arrange a place and time to meet and start on our trip. We finally agreed to meet on top of Iron Mountain, where the road passes through a gap, on Saturday night, at ten o'clock, September 28. After these arrangements had been completed and it was all understood, we spent the last week visiting around among our friends at night and having a good time generally.

My leave of absence had expired, and I knew my Lieutenant was looking for me, and expecting me every day, but that did not disturb me in the least.

There was a disposition on the part of some of the boys to commit depredations of some kind on what few rebels lived around in that part of the country, in way of revenge for the many mean things they had done to them; but the majority of us counseled against it, for the reason that we were leaving friends behind, and when we were gone they would be made to suffer the more for anything we might do.

It was almost impossible to control fifteen or twenty young men burning for revenge, especially when they had suffered what these men had. They expressed no desire to take any one's life but they did want to do something that would make their enemies remember them, and a great many things were suggested. I will here relate one suggestion that was carried into effect. I simply relate this incident to show their temper, and how determined they were to do some mischief. In the neighborhood lived a man by the name of Robinson. He owned a nice farm in the valley, just one mile from Mountain City. He was a cattle fancier, and claimed to have some very fine stock, and among them a blooded bull that he prized very highly. He was the only rebel save one in the neighborhood. One day there were twenty or twenty-five of us together and in order to appease our thirst for tragedy, and to satisfy our longing to seek some kind of mild revenge, we decided that on that night we would hang Robinson's bull. We procured a sheet or two of legal cap, and prepared a document purporting to be his will, gathered up some ropes and log chains from different places, and about ten o'clock at night started for Robinson's farm, and hanged the bull to an old apple tree. We then tacked the document containing his will in the middle of his forehead, and left, feeling that our thirst for blood had been satisfied.

Many times in later years I have thought of this incident, and wondered why we did it. That apple tree is standing to-day in that orchard, and is noted and known all over the country as being the tree on which Robinson's bull was hanged.

It was a hazardous trip, but I believe I could make it.

FROM THE NATIONAL TRIBUNE, JAN 4, 1900

As the time for us to start was drawing near, I decided to visit my home once more, and while I knew it was hazardous, I believed with the proper precaution that I could make the trip. Some of my comrades insisted that I ought not undertake it, but I felt sure I could do it. So on Wednesday afternoon before the time set to start on Saturday night, I started to my father's house, following the summit of the mountains. I shortened the distance many miles from that of the road, which ran around the base of the mountains. Night settled down about the time I crossed the summit of the Allegheny Mountains, but being used to hardships, and familiar with the path that led through that dense forest, I hurried on and made rapid time. About ten o'clock I reached my old home at the back of the farm.

I hurried through the fields and down the path leading to the barn — the little path I had so often traveled over in my childhood days. I cautiously approached the barn, made an examination to see if any strange horses were there, and finding everything all right, I softly slipped through the back gate and up the path to the house, made an alarm at the door, and was admitted. Father and mother were much surprised at my presence, as well as alarmed, and asked me what in the world I was doing there, when I knew I was in danger of being killed; told me the authorities there had just heard of my desertion, and they would make a greater effort than ever before to get me. I reassured them and quieted their fears, telling them my plans. Then I said good-by for the last time, turned, and hurried through the back door, down by the barn, out along the little path along the hillside, and was soon in the woods. By noon I had arrived at my destination among my friends. I was tired and worn out, and lay down and slept till night, and was not yet rested from my long, hard trip across the mountains. I did not go out with the boys, but slept all night, and next morning was fully rested, and felt equal for any emergency that might happen.

My story would not be complete were I not to relate the circumstance that occurred the night before we set out. During the day I received a note from Miss Edith Carroll, who, the reader will remember, figured in the first part of this story in my first arrest. She had sent the note by an old man, a good friend of mine, and who knew me well. He lived less than a mile from her father's house, where I was first captured. He was also a good Union man. She requested that I meet her at the house of the bearer of the note at from 10 to 11 o'clock that night. She had something important to tell me, and I must not fail to be there.

Knowing that her sympathies were with the South, I hesitated. I did not want to make any mistake, and fall into a trap just when the way was clear for my escape. I asked the old man if he thought it would be perfectly safe for me to go. He said he was sure it was. Said he: "The girl seems to be very much excited about something, and said she must see you. Come to-night at 11 o'clock, and I will stand guard, so there will be no possibility of your falling into a trap."

"Tell her I will be there at 11 o'clock to-night."

I procured a horse that was fairly fast of foot. I had about six or seven miles to go. About 10 o'clock at night, after disguising myself to the extent that anyone meeting me in the dark along the road would not recognize me, I mounted my horse and was soon dashing across the country at a rapid pace.

I was dashing across the country at a rapid pace.
FROM THE NATIONAL TRIBUNE, JAN 11, 1900

THE ADVENTURES OF A CONSCRIPT

I arrived at the place at about the time designated. They were expecting me. The old gentleman and Miss Edith met me at the gate. The old man said he would sit and hold my horse, and give the alarm should any danger appear, and Miss Edith could tell me what she desired to see me for.

We walked to the house, were shown into the sitting room, and left alone.

Miss Edith said: "I am so delighted to see you. I heard last night that you had again deserted and was in this part of the country. I heard it from Maj. Long, who captured you a year ago at my father's house. He came to see me and wanted me to assist in your capture; said there was a reward offered for you, and if I would become a party to your capture he would share it with me. And he suggested that I scheme to meet you at my home or any place you might designate, with the understanding that he be concealed with a squad of men and surround and capture you. Further, he said when they get you again you would never give them or any one else any more trouble. I knew what he meant, and those words went like an arrow to my heart. I remembered that at our parting a year ago I registered a vow in Heaven to protect you in every way I could. I spurned his offer, told him I was not doing that kind of business, and even if I was I doubted very much my ability to accomplish your capture. He swore with an oath that he would never rest till he got you. This threat at once became a great burden to me, and I determined to see you, but did not know how it was possible for me to do so until I at last conceived the idea that I have just carried out: and I dare not let my family know anything about this. I slipped from my room an hour ago, and they do not know I am away."

I thanked the young lady heartily for her interest, and assured her that I felt sure of escaping this time to the Union lines.

After some further conversation I arose to start. She walked down to the gate with me, where the old man was holding my horse. I took him by the hand and bade him good-bye, and he turned and walked to the house. "And now," said I, "Miss Edith, again I thank you for your kindness," and taking her by the hand said good-bye. Holding my hand she said:

"May the God in whom we trust guide and protect you." Then, mounting my horse, I was soon flying across the country on my way back. It was now about midnight, and I soon arrived among my friends.

The next day was Saturday, our last day there. We spent the day visiting our friends and bidding then good-bye, and as the evening shadows began to gather along the valley, we moved in crowds for our meeting place on the mountain, two or three miles away. Myself and those with me arrived there long before 10 o'clock but they soon began to gather in from all directions, and when 10 o'clock had come we lined them up and counted them. We found we had just eighty-five ready to start.

We traveled all night as fast as we could, and when daylight came we would inquire of the Union people along the road as to the probability of there being any danger ahead. The best information we could get the way was clear. The rebel army lay some distance to our right. We were keeping close to the base of the mountains, and the only danger we feared was that we might be reported to the Confederates, and cavalry might dash across the country and head us off.

About 2 o'clock in the afternoon we came up with two Union scouts who were perfectly familiar with the country. We placed ourselves in their hands, for the reason that they could lead us to the nearest route into the Union lines. We were all extremely tired, and some nearly given out. We went down in a deep ravine some distance from the road and lay down, and rested perhaps two hours. The scouts said it was yet twenty to twenty-five miles to the Union army by the nearest way we could go, and we would have to double-quick a portion of the way. They said the rebels were maneuvering on our right, and extending their lines east in front of us, but we would have no trouble to flank them when dark came. So after we had rested we again started on our home stretch.

It was a long, hard pull. I am sure I was never so tired in my life as I was that evening about dark. And to add to my suffering my feet were almost a solid blister on the soles. I thought several times I could get no further, and I was not alone; others were in the same fix. I shall never forget the suffering of that night, and had it not been that the goal of my ambition was but a few miles ahead of us, I would have lain down by the roadside and given it up.

We traveled on till about 2 o'clock in the morning, when we came up to the Union pickets. The two scouts advanced and reported. The officer in charge lined his men up by the roadside, and we marched past in double file, while the guard stood at present arms.

We marched into the town of Jonesboro,[45] or the edge of the town rather, where we found a large old barn, and we all found a place in it to lie down, and being so tired and exhausted were soon asleep.

We slept till daylight, when we began to get up and look around. We started up town altogether, and the first thing that attracted our attention was the flag — the Old Stars and Stripes, floating over the courthouse.

The boys began to cheer. We formed them in line double file, and marched around the courthouse square, cheering and hallooing like wild men.

I shall never forget the sensation that came over me when I looked down that line of men, who had suffered so long and so much, some cheering, some throwing their hats and others weeping like children. Poor fellows, it seemed that their joy had no bounds, and they cheered until they were so hoarse they were forced to stop.

This was Monday morning the 30th of September, and it marks an epoch in the history of my life. We reached the Union army none too soon for our safety. About nine o'clock orders were given to fall back to Greenville, about twenty-five miles, and we at once

---

[45] Jonesboro was originally founded as Jonesborough, but had shortened the name over time. In the 1980s, the town reverted the spelling to Jonesborough.

started on the march. We arrived there on Tuesday morning and began to make arrangements to enlist and organize our company for the Union service.[46]

Jonesboro Courthouse as it appeared during the Civil War.

FROM THE COLLECTION OF THE JONESBOROUGH/WASHINGTON COUNTY HISTORY MUSEUM AND ARCHIVES, OPERATED BY THE HERITAGE ALLIANCE, JONESBOROUGH, TENNESSEE.

---

[46] According to W. H. Younce's obituary, after applying, it was recommended by a Colonel that he instead go to Indiana. Two members of the Indiana Infantry (who were brothers from Franklin), suggested he go to Franklin. He arrived soon after, in October 1863.

EPILOGUE

It has not been my purpose in writing this story to revive any of the animosities of the Civil War. I thank God that the wounds left by that struggle are healed. The bloody chasm is closed, and the tramp of the warrior and the clangor of arms no longer echo on our mountains or in our valleys. The garments dyed in blood have passed away, and we live to enjoy the rich boon of freedom and prosperity, purchased with the blood of the thousands of patriots who found their last resting place amid the thunderbolts of war, 'neath the whispering pines and palmettos of the South-land, and that we are again one Nation, one people, under one flag. But few men living to-day have greater wrongs to forgive than myself; but I have tried to forgive them as I hope to be forgiven. All the characters mentioned in this story are real and true to name, except the Carroll family.

Edith Carroll is an assumed name for a real character. A short time after the close of the war she was happily married and is now the mother of a grown-up family, though I have never seen her since that midnight parting before mentioned, on the night before my departure for the Union army. A few years ago I visited that country where the scenes and incidents involved in this story took place. Nearly all the parties mentioned have passed from earth into the great unknown. I know of but two or three besides myself that are left. That father and mother on whose souls this great burden of anguish and sorrow fell heaviest are peacefully sleeping side by side in the old churchyard on the hill-side, "in the windowless palace of the dead." Storms may mutter around that lone and silent resting-place, and fields run red with other wars; they are at rest.[47] But few of the friends of my youth are there, and only the hands of strangers greet me in my native land. Those whom I loved in childhood are scattered here and there, and many have passed over the dark river of death and gone from earth forever.

---

[47] An allusion to Robert Green Ingersoll's speeches of 1876 and 1888.

APPENDIX

CENSUS RECORDS

Year	Name	Age	Occupation	Birth State
1850	David Younce	36	Farming	TN
	Lois Younce	42	-	NC
	Susan Younce	18	-	NC
	Sarah Younce	15	-	NC
	Calvin Younce	12	-	NC
	William Younce	9	-	NC
	Minerva Younce	5	-	NC
1860	David Younce	47	Farming	NC
	Lois Younce	53	-	NC
	Calvin Younce	21	-	NC
	William Younce	18	-	NC
	Minerva Younce	15	-	NC
1870	William H. Younce	27	School Teacher	NC
	Lizzie Younce	27	Keeping House	KY
	Alice Younce	4	-	IN
1880	Buck Younce	42	Shoe Merchant	NC
	Elizabeth Younce	35	Keeping House	IN
	Alice Younce	13	-	IN
	1890 Census Records Destroyed			
1900	William H. Younce	58	Merchant: Shoes & Boots	NC
	Elizabeth Younce	56	Keeping House	KY
	Juda A. Terhune	86	-	KY
1910	William H. Younce	67	Retail Shoe Store	NC
	Elizabeth A, Younce	66	-	KY
1920	W.H. Younce	77	Retired	NC
	Elizabeth A. Younce	76	-	KY
	W.V. Slack	48	Salesman	TN
	Alice Slack	48	-	IN

Based on a review of census records, and birth and death certificates, David and Lois Younce had six children: Nancy, Susan, Sarah, Calvin, William, and Minerva.

Nancy and Susan were twins, born in 1832, and they married brothers, John Brown and Benjamin Brown, respectively. Notably, John served in the 58th North Carolina Infantry, and Benjamin served in the 21st Virginia Cavalry, which are the same two units as W. H. described in his adventures.

Benjamin was shot in battle in Virginia two days before Lee's surrender in April 1865. He succumbed to his wounds in May. Susan later married Enoch Lewis. Susan passed away in 1916 in Ashe County, North Carolina.

Nancy lived until 1929, reaching the age of 97, in Ashe County.

Sarah, also known as "Sallie," was born in 1835. She married Wilburn Robinson and passed away in 1929 in Lee County, Virginia.

Calvin, born in 1839, married Mary, nicknamed "Mollie" Jackson. He died in 1926 in Bristol, Tennessee.

Unfortunately, no additional records on Minerva Younce have been found after her appearance in the 1850 and 1860 censuses.

William, after the war, settled in Franklin, Indiana. He married Elizabeth Terhune in 1865. In the 1870 census, W. H. appeared alongside his wife and their daughter Alice. During this census, he was listed as a school teacher. However, starting with the 1880 census, his occupation was recorded as a shoe salesman. By the 1920 census, Alice, and her husband William Slack, had moved into the house with W. H. and Elizabeth.

W. H. became a successful businessman and prominent citizen. He served on the Johnson County Board of Education from 1897 to 1902, including one year as Superintendent, and two terms on the city council. In 1890, he helped found the Franklin Mutual Building & Loan, now known as the Mutual Savings Bank of Franklin, and served for 25 years as its first president.

In 1881, W. H. opened his shoe store in downtown Franklin. The Franklin Evening Star published advertisements for the store between July 1914 and October 1915. Photos of the store appear on the next page.

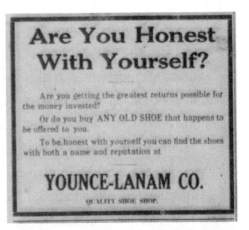

PHOTOGRAPHS COURTESY
OF THE JOHNSON COUNTY
HISTORICAL SOCIETY AND
MUSEUM OF HISTORY,
FRANKLIN, INDIANA.

Younce Shoe Store was located at 34 West Jefferson Street in Franklin, while the Younce home stood at 148 North Main Street. Although both buildings no longer exist, their footprints can be placed on current aerial imagery using the locations found on a 1927 fire insurance map in the archives of the Johnson County Museum of History. Presently, the county courthouse building occupies the former store location, while the house has been replaced by a parking lot.

| | | | | | Store | | Projection: Mercator |

0   50   100   200   ☐ Store   Projection: Mercator
                                 ☐ House   Data sources: Esri, Johnson County
              Feet

A few months before W.H. passed away, the Masonic Temple was built across the street from the Younce house. A photograph taken at the temple's groundbreaking ceremony in March 1922 shows the Younce house in the center background. Coincidentally, the Masonic Temple building now houses the Johnson County Museum of History..

PORTRAIT OF WILLIAM HENRY YOUNCE

YOUNCE STREET

Younce Street, a road running through Franklin's Lynhurst neighborhood, was constructed around the 1940s. Houses line the street, and at one end sits the Little League ballpark. While no records have been located regarding the specific reasons for its naming, it is believed that the street was dedicated to recognize W. H. Younce for his many years of service in Franklin.

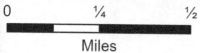
Miles

Projection: Mercator
Data sources: Esri, Johnson County

By W. H. YOUNCE, Late 58th N. C.

On November 23, 1899, The National Tribune, a newspaper for veterans, printed the first of eight weekly installments from W. H.'s memoirs. Each article featured the above header and included a drawing depicting a scene from the story. The first four articles were published on the front page.

In 1901, W. H. compiled the eight articles and published his memoirs as a book. The Editor Publishing Company in Cincinnati, Ohio, handled the printing. A copy of the completed book was held by the New York Public Library, which scanned and provided it to the Internet Archive.[48]

In 2022, this second edition of the book was printed, marking 121 years since the first edition and exactly one century following W. H.'s death.

---

[48] Source: https://archive.org/details/adventuresofcons00youn

LEGACY

Newspaper articles document the subsequent lives of W. H. and his family.

W. H. returned to the South at least three times. He visited his brother Calvin in Tennessee in 1890, which was his first visit since the Civil War. He made two additional trips in 1910 and 1912.

In early 1918, W. H. retired from the shoe business, and an announcement appeared in the Franklin Evening Star.

Four years after his retirement, on May 27, 1922, William Henry Younce passed away in Franklin. His obituary was published in the May 29th edition of the Franklin Evening Star.

Elizabeth passed away two years later, on September 7, 1924. Her obituary appeared in the Franklin Evening Star the following day.

As for the remaining family, Alice married William V. Slack at the Younce home in 1891. William Slack was the son of a Tennessee newspaper publisher and state senator.

Alice and William had one child, a son named Celete, who, by all accounts, was as an intelligent young man. He displayed early talent as an amateur magician, and numerous stories were printed about his successful escapes from handcuffs and even jail cells.

Tragically, Celete died in 1911 at the age of 18 due to an accidental self-inflicted gunshot while attempting a magic trick.

William died in 1935, leaving Alice as the last survivor. Alice passed away in 1957. Her obituary was published in the Franklin Evening Star on June 17th, marking the end of the line for the descendants of William H. Younce.

Jul 11, 1890 - Franklin Republican

Mr. W. H. Younce, wife, and daughter Miss Alice, of Franklin, Indiana are visiting Mr. Charles *[sic]* Younce and family on South Alabama Street. Messrs. Younce are brothers, and have not seen each other for twenty-five years — Bristol (Tenn.) News

Jul 1, 1892 - Franklin Republican

W.H. Younce will leave this evening for Bristol, Tennessee, to join his wife who is visiting their daughter, Mrs. W.V. Slack. From Bristol, Mr. Younce will go to other parts of Eastern Tennessee, and before returning will visit his mother in North Carolina.

Jul 13, 1912 - Franklin Evening Star

W.H. Younce will leave next Tuesday for a three weeks' trip to the south. He will make a few days' stay near Cumberland Gap, Virginia, and also at Bristol, Tenn. He expects to spend two weeks with relatives at Ashland, N.C. Mr. Younce was born at Jefferson N.C.

VETERAN SHOE DEALER RETIRES

A deal was consummated Thursday whereby W. H. Younce of the Younce-Lanam Shoe company, sold his interest to Sam Lanam and Joseph Simpson. Sam George will also take an interest in the shoe business forming a corporation, which will likely take the name of Lanam-Simpson company. Mr. Younce is Franklin's veteran shoe merchant and has been in business here forty-five years. He occupied the same location thirty-six years.

Mr. Younce is now seventy-five years old and with his retirement from business he feels that a much needed rest is due him. He started in business on a small bank account and a comfortable competency was acquired through frugality and perseverance, together with his business acumen. His first venture in the shoe business was with employment by John Hutchison who occupied the room which is the location for the J.M. Henderson store. He afterwards was employed by H.H. Luyster and George Gilchrist for five years. Mr. Younce then formed partnership with O.C. Dunn in the merchant tailoring and shoe business. Two years later, he sold his interest to Mr. Dunn and in 1880 went into business for himself. He occupied two different locations before moving in 1881 to the present location of the Younce store. Mr. Younce has made a very wide acquaintanceship over this and other counties during his business career. He was a splendid salesman and was a close student of the leather industry. Messrs. Lanam and Simpson will receive as an inheritance, a big volume of business built up by Mr. Younce which has steadily increased since the Younce-Lanam company was formed. Both are competent and industrious shoe dealers with considerable experience. The new company should have a very successful career.

W. H. YOUNCE
VETERAN, SHOE MERCHANT DEAD

Funeral Services Held This Afternoon at the Home on N. Main

William H. Younce, for almost half a century a leading shoe merchant of Franklin died Saturday afternoon at 3:30 at his home on North Main Street. Death was due to creeping paralysis which developed more than a year ago and which compelled Mr. Younce to take to his bed during July of 1921.

Escaped Confederate Army

Mr. Younce was born July 26, 1842 in Ashe County, North Carolina. Although a firm believer in the Union cause he was conscripted into the service of the Confederate army when he was eighteen years old. He escaped and sought to join the Union army but was recaptured. He escaped and was captured again. When he escaped the third time the Confederate chiefs put a price on his head dead or alive. He begged to be allowed to join the Union forces but the Colonel to whom he applied advised him to go into Indiana. He met the Dunlap brothers, father and uncle of Mrs. E. O. Collins, who were in the Union army, and they urged him to come to Franklin, which he did in October of 1863.

Engaged in Shoe Business

In August of 1865, Mr. Younce was married to Elizabeth Terhuen, daughter of William Terhune, a locally famous farmer and breeder of fancy horses. He engaged in the shoe business in 1881 with I. N. McLoughlin and continued in the business until 1918 when failing health compelled him to retire. During his career as a shoe merchant he was associated first with Mr. McLoughlin, then with Chester Payne, later with his son-in-law, William Slack and closed his business career as the head of the Younce-Lanam Shoe Company of which Sam Lanam was the junior partner.

Active in City Affairs

Mr. Younce took an active interest in the development of Franklin and served in many capacities for the upbuilding of the community. He was president of the Mutual Building & Loan Association for twenty-five years, contributing much to the establishment of the very helpful service of that association. He served as a city councilman for four years, was a member of the board of education for two terms, took an aggressive part on the local and state affairs of the Republican party and cooperated in many civic enterprises.

Mr. Younce had been a member of the Grace Methodist church for fifty-five years. He was a Mason and a member of the Knights of Pythias lodge.

Mr. Younce always was proud of the fact that he was mainly responsible for the temperance clause in the Knights of Pythias By-Laws, which provided that a dealer in liquor was ineligible for membership.

Widow and Daughter Survive

Mr. Younce is survived by his widow, and a daughter, Mrs. Will V. Slack. He also leaves a brother, Calvin Younce, who lives in Bristol, Tenn., and two sisters, Mrs. Wm. Brown, whose home is in North Carolina and Mrs. J. D. Robinson, whose home is in Tennessee.

Funeral Held This Afternoon

Burial was in Greenlawn cemetery, the casket bearers including E. C. Miller, Samuel Featherngill, J. M. Robinson, Dr. James Richardson, O. I. Jones and O. L. Vandivier. The Knights of Pythias Lodge will conduct services at the cemetery.

MRS. ELIZABETH YOUNCE DIES SUDDENLY FROM HEART ATTACK SUNDAY

Well Known Woman Had Fractured Hip in Fall Few Weeks Ago

The death of Mrs. Elizabeth Terhune Younce, widow of the late W. H. Younce and mother of Mrs. Will V. Slack, occurred at the home on North Main Street Sunday morning at 6 o'clock. News of the death came as a shock to the many friends in this city who were encouraged by her favorable recovery from a fractured hip which she sustained a few months ago, but an attack of heart trouble, following comfortable night's rest aroused the family and death soon resulted.

Born in Kentucky

Mrs. Younce was born in Harrodsburg. Ky., Oct. 1, 1843, and when a young girl came with her parents. William and Judda Terhune, to Johnson County and resided in the Hopewell community where she attended school. On August 8, 1865, she was married to the late W. H. Younce and their entire life was spent in Franklin where Mr. Younce was a successful business man. His death occurred two years ago.

Mrs. Younce was one of the oldest members of the Grace Methodist Church and their home has always been opened to those who ministered and served the church during these years. In her quiet, gentle, sweet-spirited manner, she endeared herself to those who knew her. The affection between mother and daughter. Mrs. Alice Younce Slack, was beautiful. and both Mr. and Mrs. Slack were untiring in their devotion and care for her.

Funeral services will be held at the home. Tuesday afternoon at 2:30 o'clock. The Rev. C. P. Gibbs of the Methodist Church will be in charge of ha services. Burial will be made in Greenlawn Cemetery.

There was a Christmas Eve wedding at the residence of W. H. Younce in our city when Miss Alice Younce and Will V. Slack, of Bristol, Tenn. were married by Rev. E. H. Wood in the presence of a few invited guests. The happy couple left for the home of the groom the next day where he is employed in a railroad office. The best wishes of a large circle of friends are extended for their future happiness.

YOUTHFUL ENTERTAINERS APPEAR AT Y.M.C.A. SHOW

Charles Metzger and Celete B. Slack Win Applause by Clever Work With Shackles.

"Marvelo" was the title of an entertainment given at Y.M.C.A. auditorium last night when Charles Metzger, son of Chief Metzger, and his partner, Celete B. Slack, appeared as the star performers. They delivered themselves from handcuffs, chains, shackles, and straight-jackets in remarkably quick time and their clever work won applause from an audience of 200 persons.

E. H. Habig and E. G. Crabb, older and more experienced than the "jail breaking" artists, were entertaining in ball, plate, and Indian Club juggling. Wood Nichols and Earl Twinkle, F.E. McCormick and Hugh Shields had places on the program. Music was furnished by the colored Y.M.C.A. orchestra. The proceeds will be used in sending boys to the Lake Geneva conference. The Y.M.C.A. members who made the successful performance possible were Frank Cantrell, general manager; Robert Koogle, advertising agent: Roy Wensley, stage manager; Harry Hauger, electrician; Carl Bittrich, property man; S.A. Ratliff, musical director; Wood Nichols, head usher; A.K. Jones, treasurer.

AUGUST 24 1911 - INDIANAPOLIS NEWS

SHOOTS HIMSELF WHILE TRYING TRICK OF MAGIC

CELETE B. SLACK, INDIANAPOLIS STUDENT, IS DEAD.

OUTING HAS TRAGIC ENDING

Celete B. Slack, eighteen years old, a well known young Indianapolis student. brought a tragic end to a jest, when he placed a revolver to his head and pulled the trigger, yesterday afternoon, at the country hotel of George Shay, in the National road, near Greenfield. He was killed almost instantly. Slack thought he had moved the cylinder of his weapon until the plunger of the trigger was on an empty chamber and he remarked that he would pull the trigger and not fire the gun. He fell before the eyes of several friends.

On Veranda of Hotel

The accident occurred on the veranda of the hotel. Slack had been spending a vacation week at the Shay place and Miss Blanche O'Nell, Charles Metzger and Wilbert Hunt, young friends from Indianapolis, had gone to the place to spend the day. Slack and the other young men had been Interested for some time in sleight of hand and tricks of magic. Watched carefully by the others he toyed with the revolver, loading the cylinder apparently carefully. Them he twirled it, and in answer to a caution from the young woman remarked;

"I can shoot and not shoot- see?" And with that he placed the weapon against his head and pulled the trigger.

Slack's parents are making their home in Denver. His grandfather, W. H. Younce, of Franklin. Ind., was called to the farm at once. Dispatches were sent to the parents, and they are on their way to Indianapolis. Robert Metzger, former chief of police, was called to the Shay place by his son Charles.

The family is well known in Indianapolis, which was its home until recently. The dead young man finished a course at Manual Training high school two years ago, and had taken a short course at Franklin College, in preparation for Harvard university, which he planned to enter this fall. Slack was regarded as a brilliant student.

Practiced Many Tricks

Slack. and Metzger had gained some fame among friends and companions by exhibitions of sleight of hand. The boys were often about central police station when Metzger's father was chief, and when a "Jail breaker" from a local vaudeville theater called at police station to show ability to open locks the boys were careful observers and repeated the feats.

The body of the young man was taken in charge by his grandfather, and was taken to the latter's home in Franklin.

WILLIAM V. SLACK, 63, DIES AT METHODIST HOSPITAL SATURDAY

Former Franklin Business Man
Had Been Ill For Past Five Years

William V. Slack, age 63, former well known Franklin business man and a resident of Franklin for the past 43 years, died Saturday morning at 1 o'clock at the Methodist hospital in Indianapolis, where he had been a patient for the past six weeks.

Mr. Slack was taken to the hospital for treatment for a condition brought about as the result of a stroke of paralysis about five years ago and his condition was not regarded as particularly serious at the time.

Several days ago pneumonia developed and he was placed in an oxygen tent and his condition seemed to improve, but Friday he became worse and he gradually grew weaker until his death Saturday morning.

Funeral Monday

The body was brought to the Flinn mortuary Saturday morning, and will remain there until Sunday afternoon when it will be taken to the home on North Main Street where friends may call at any time after 2:30 o'clock.

Funeral services will be held Monday afternoon at 2:30 o'clock at the residence, 148 North Main Street, in charge of the Rev. E. E. Aldrich, pastor of the Grace M.E. Church. Burial in Greenlawn cemetery.

Mr. Slack was born on June 10, 1872 in Bristol, Tenn., and was a son of John and Julia Penelope Slack. He was united in marriage to Miss Alice Younce of Franklin in 1891, and to them one son was born, Celete, who died in 1911. The death of the only son, a brilliant young man, was a tragedy to his parents, as he was just entering the threshold of an active business life and gave great promise for a successful future.

Engaged in Shoe Business

Mr. Slack was engaged in the retail shoe business in Franklin for many years, being associated with his father-in-law, the late W. H. Younce. After disposing of his interests in the shoe store, Mr. Slack was a traveling salesman for a large shoe manufacturing company for several years and had a wide acquaintance among shoe dealers of Indiana and the Middlewest.

Following a stroke of paralysis five years ago, Mr. Slack had been forced to retire and he had been a semi-invalid during that period.

In addition to the widow, Mr. Slack is survived by one brother and five sisters. The brother, E. M. Slack, is a well known newspaper publisher of Bristol, Tenn. and is a graduate of Franklin college. The sisters are Mrs. B.K. Middleton of Oklahoma City; Mrs. Laura M. Boden, of Johnson City, Tenn.; Mrs. William Ray, of Bristol, Tenn.; Mrs. J. R. Robb of Chicago; and Mrs. Georgia Sawtelle, of Topeka, Kan.

Was Leading Churchman

Mr. Slack was a leading member of the Grace Methodist church and was active in all departments of church work during his residence in Franklin. Following the burning of the church building about five years ago, Mr. Slack was named chairman of the committee to rebuild the church.

He gave most freely of his time to that work, and the remodeling and rebuilding were well under way when he suffered the stroke that took him from active service. His fine contribution to the church is shown today in the beautiful edifice which he helped to plan and build.

Mr. Slack was also a member of the Knights of Pythias and Masonic lodges of Franklin.

JUNE 17, 1957 - FRANKLIN EVENING STAR

ALICE YOUNT*[sic]* SLACK DIES AT HOME HERE

Funeral Services To Be Held Wednesday

Death came suddenly to Mrs. Alice Younce Slack, widow of William V. Slack, a former shoe dealer of Franklin, at her home, 148 North Main Street, at 9:15 o'clock Monday morning. Mrs. Slack had not been in good health for several years, but had been able to sit in her chair and watch television Sunday night. Funeral services have been arranged for Wednesday afternoon at 2 o'clock and will be in her home. Dr. Robert Baldridge, pastor of the Grace Methodist church, will be in charge of the services and burial will be made in Greenlawn Cemetery The body will be taken to the Slack home where friends may call Tuesday afternoon and evening and again on Wednesday until time for the services. They are invited to attend the rites. It was Mrs Slack's request no flowers be sent.

Born in County

The daughter of the late William H. and Elizabeth Terhune Younce. Mrs. Slack was born in Johnson County and, with the exception of short time following her marriage. when they resided in Tennessee, had always made her home here. Mrs. Slack had attended the Franklin schools and was a graduate of Franklin High School. In her early years prior to her marriage, she had been a teacher in the school at Hopewell. She became the bride of Mr. Slack and a son, Celete, was born to them. He died at the age of 18 years. Mr. Slack died March 30. 1935. Mrs. Slack was a member of the Grace Methodist church. Second cousins are the only survivors.

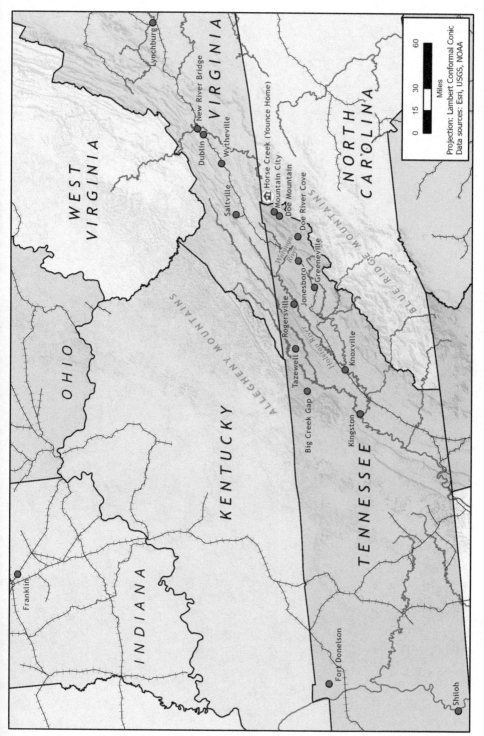

Made in the USA
Las Vegas, NV
03 September 2024

94708465R00079